Effective Provision for
Able & Talented
Children

Barry Teare

Published by Network Educational Press Ltd.
PO Box 635
Stafford
ST16 1BF

First Published 1997
Re-printed 1999
© Barry Teare 1997

ISBN 1 85539 041 8

Barry Teare asserts the moral right to be identified
as the author of this work

Series Editor - Professor Tim Brighouse
Edited by Carol Thompson
Design & layout by
Neil Hawkins of Devine Design
Illustrations by Joe Rice

Printed in Great Britain by
Redwood Books, Trowbridge, Wilts.

Foreword

A teacher's task is much more ambitious than it used to be and demands a focus on the subtleties of teaching and learning and on the emerging knowledge of school improvement.

This is what this series is about.

Teaching can be a very lonely activity. The time honoured practice of a single teacher working alone in the classroom is still the norm; yet to operate alone is, in the end to become isolated and impoverished. This series addresses two issues – the need to focus on practical and useful ideas connected with teaching and learning and the wish thereby to provide some sort of an antidote to the loneliness of the long distance teacher who is daily berated by an anxious society.

Teachers flourish best when, in key stage teams or departments (or more rarely whole schools), their talk is predominantly about teaching and learning and where, unconnected with appraisal, they are privileged to observe each other teach; to plan and review their work together; and to practise the habit of learning from each other new teaching techniques. But how does this state of affairs arise? Is it to do with the way staffrooms are physically organised so that the walls bear testimony to interesting articles and in the corner there is a dedicated computer tuned to 'conferences' about SEN, school improvement, the teaching of English etc., and whether, in consequence, the teacher leaning over the shoulder of the enthusiastic IT colleagues sees the promise of interesting practice elsewhere? Has the primary school cracked it when it organises successive staff meetings in different classrooms and invites the 'host' teacher to start the meeting with a 15 minute exposition of their classroom organisation and management? Or is it the same staff sharing, on a rota basis, a slot on successive staff meeting agenda when each in turn reviews a new book they have used with their class? And what of the whole school which now uses 'active' and 'passive' concerts of carefully chosen music as part of their accelerated learning techniques?

It is of course well understood that excellent teachers feel threatened when first they are observed. Hence the epidemic of trauma associated with OFSTED. The constant observation of the teacher in training seems like that of the learner driver. Once you have passed your test and can drive unaccompanied, you do. You often make lots of mistakes and sometimes get into bad habits. Woe betide, however, the back seat driver who tells you so. In the same way the new teacher quickly loses the habit of observing others and being observed. So how do we get a confident, mutual observation debate going? One school I know found a simple and therefore brilliant solution. The Head of the History Department asked that a young colleague plan lessons for her – the Head of Department – to teach. This lesson she then taught, and was observed by the young colleague. There was subsequent discussion, in which the young teacher asked,

> *"Why did you divert the question and answer session I had planned?"*
> *and was answered by,*
> *"Because I could see that I needed to arrest the attention of the group by the window with some "hands-on" role play, etc."*

This lasted an hour and led to a once-a-term repeat discussion which, in the end, was adopted by the whole school. The whole school subsequently changed the pattern of its meetings to consolidate extended debate about teaching and learning. The two teachers claimed that because one planned and the other taught both were implicated but neither alone was responsible or felt 'got at'.

So there are practices which are both practical and more likely to make teaching a rewarding and successful activity. They can, as it were, increase the likelihood of a teacher surprising the pupils into understanding or doing something they did not think they could do rather than simply entertaining them or worse still occupying them. There are ways of helping teachers judge the best method of getting pupil expectation just ahead of self-esteem.

This series focuses on straightforward interventions which individual schools and teachers use to make life more rewarding for themselves and those they teach. Teachers deserve nothing less, for they are the architects of tomorrow's society, and society's ambition for what they achieve increases as each year passes.

Professor Tim Brighouse.

Contents

INTRODUCTION

> "If you have great talents, industry will improve them...."

Sir Joshua Reynolds, 1723-1792, **'Discourses, 2'** as quoted in **'The Penguin Dictionary of Quotations'**, *J M & M J Cohen (Bloomsbury Books, 1960)*

> "Everybody has the ability and can use it without being scared of being bullied because of it."

Part of evaluation sheet of an enrichment session by a Year 9 pupil, June 1996.

Why should provision be made?

For the children themselves

All children, including the most able, have a right to a challenging and appropriate education. There have been far too many instances of able and talented children being left unfulfilled, bored, underchallenged or frightened to use their abilities for fear of peer pressure. Ruth Railton, writing the story of the National Youth Orchestra, took her title **'Daring to Excel'** *(Secker and Warburg, 1992)* from:

> The danger chiefly lies in acting well;
> No crime's so great as daring to excel.

Charles Churchill, **'Epistle to William Hogarth'**, 1763

Those of us in education have to ensure that able and talented children have sufficient opportunities to use their abilities and that they are encouraged to excel.

For other children

Evidence from OFSTED supports the view that if schools are willing and able to meet the needs of able pupils, standards are raised for all pupils (as stated by Mike Tomlinson, Director of Inspection at Easthamstead, Berkshire on 20th June 1995).

Children are the most important part of the equation. Effective provision for able and talented pupils helps not only them but their classmates as well.

For teachers

Caring for children, all children, nurturing them and assisting them to achieve what they are capable of doing is central to the teaching role. Not to do the best for all pupils, including the most able, would be to neglect one's professional duty.

For parents

The great majority of parents are anxious that their children are happy at school and that they are progressing well. The National Association for Gifted Children (NAGC) receives distressing letters from parents telling of problems of inadequate provision which leaves the child unhappy and which has damaging 'knock-on' effects upon the rest of the family. As parents say, their children only get the one schooling, which needs to be challenging and rich.

For the wellbeing of the school
In recent years schools have come under much greater scrutiny. They are certainly more accountable. All schools need a fair proportion of able pupils but to keep them and to encourage others to join them, they need to make effective provision. Otherwise many families will 'vote with their feet'. The OFSTED process has given attention to this issue and provision for able and talented children has been included in the Key Issues for Action for many schools. This attention is one part of a wider concern over standards and school effectiveness. In what is becoming a much more market-led situation, schools have to compete for a healthy intake and one which includes a reasonable number of the most able.

What are the necessary steps in effective provision?

- **An understanding of the necessary theory**
- **A whole school policy**
- **Departmental policies and procedures**
- **Inservice work**
- **Resourcing**
- **Lead from a co-ordinator**
- **Identification**
- **Classroom strategies and extra-curricular provision**
- **Monitoring and evaluation**

All these points will be discussed in detail in later sections.

A higher profile
Provision for able and talented children was very much a "Cinderella" area in the past – not properly looked after nor valued. Often it was seen, mistakenly, as elitist. There is now a much higher national profile which is causing pressure for action.

There have been major developments nationally:

1. The 1992 HMI publication **"The Education Of Very Able Children In Maintained Schools"** recognised progress but also pointed the way to further necessary improvements.
2. **The 1993 Governors Guide to the Law** recommended that schools should include arrangements for very able children in the curriculum statement.
3. In June 1994 the DfEE recommended that details of arrangements for the identification of very able pupils and the provision for them should be included in the school prospectus.
4. Recognition that some exceptionally able children may need to work on material from a higher key stage was included in an enabling statement in the National Curriculum.
5. OFSTED has placed additional emphasis upon the correct provision for able and talented children.

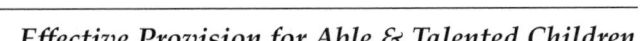

6. In 1995 the DfEE combined with the National Association for Able Children In Education to produce a booklet by Deborah Eyre, "**School Governors And More Able Children**". The booklet has been used increasingly in governor training.

7. The publication in July 1995 of "**Sport: Raising The Game**" (Department of National Heritage) put the spotlight on measures to encourage and promote sport, including the creation of a British Academy of Sport as the pinnacle of a network of centres of sporting excellence. The report also highlights the need for the Sports Council's governing bodies to set targets for ensuring that talent is identified and supported.

8. "**Setting The Scene: The Arts and Young People**", (Department of National Heritage, July 1996), stated:

"Our aim should be to spark an interest in, and enjoyment of, the arts as early in a child's life as possible, and then nurture that throughout the child's educational career. Most of us form our attitudes to life, and develop our talents and skills, while at school. It is vital therefore that schools are able to offer opportunities in the arts which are open to all pupils, and that they enable those who wish to pursue a particular talent or creative ability to do so".

The document looks to promote the arts including "training for excellence".

At the top of the political agenda.

Recently there have been some very important developments:

1. OFSTED commissioned Joan Freeman to write "**Educating the Very Able**", looking at research in this country and elsewhere. It was published in 1998.

2. In 1998 the DfEE established an Advisory Group on Gifted and Talented Children.

3. In the school year 1998-9, ten schools won bids to run masterclasses.

4. In spring 1999 came an announcement of a pilot scheme of summer schools for later in the year.

5. The ongoing review of the National Curriculum is likely to result in additional advice by QCA on provision for gifted and talented pupils.

6. In March 1999, the initiative "**Excellence In Cities**" contained steps to be taken in regard to able pupils in six major conurbations –
   - materials for able children within the National Literacy and Numeracy strategies
   - a distinct teaching and learning programme
   - in secondary schools, the appointment of a co-ordinator who is a senior member of staff
   - masterclasses, study support provision, extra teaching, summer schools, weekends
   - partnerships with independent schools
   - university summer schools
   - world-class tests

7. In April 1999 came the publication of the House of Commons Education and Employment Committee report on **"Highly Able Children"**. More than forty recommendations included –
   - a named person should be appointed by each school and each local education authority to take responsibility for highly able children
   - greater emphasis on able children within teacher training
   - greater flexibility within the Literacy Hour
   - more targeted funding
   - important opportunities for use by able children within information technology
8. September 1999 will see the reintroduction of the probationary year for teachers. NQTs will be expected to meet the challenge of the able child.

In conclusion

Some readers will be aware of recent developments, others not. All people involved in education need to take note of these and act accordingly. The wishes of official bodies, however important, are not the real driving force behind this book and its contents. We wish to proceed further because:

WE CARE ABOUT CHILDREN. WE WANT TO SEE THEM HAPPY, BUT CHALLENGED, INDIVIDUALS WITHIN A COMMUNITY, CONFIDENT TO DEVELOP THEIR ABILITIES TO THE FULL WITHOUT FEAR OF PREJUDICE AND ENVY.

As Beverley Eley commented through her sub-title to 'The Book of David' (Harper Collins, 1996), – the story of the musician David Helfgott, also made into the film 'Shine':

"It's alright to be different"

Section One

Theory into practice

In this section you will see that:

➡ educational practice needs to be based upon relevant theory and research evidence

➡ there is particularly valuable evidence to look at in the 1992 HMI review, the National Curriculum and the twelve OFSTED subject booklets

➡ a whole school policy leading to procedures involving referrals, Individual Education Plans and a register of able pupils is needed to convert theory into practice

➡ lessons from everyday life often have a transfer value and an application for effective provision

➡ theory converted by procedures into practice should answer the needs of able pupils

Many educational writers suggest that the theoretical base for practice in this country is not as strong as it could be or should be. This book is essentially practical and the weight of text is overwhelmingly on the side of what needs to *happen*. Even so it is important that those involved with the teaching and learning of the able and talented have some theory and research evidence upon which to base their policies.

Theory

In what areas do we need to develop knowledge and expertise?

- What is meant by ability both generally and specifically?
- How do we measure ability through tests and other means?
- What are the parameters when using tests?
- How do able children learn? Is this process any different from that of the majority of children?
- What does research teach us about the most sensible ways of carrying out grouping policy?
- What do longitudinal case studies, following children's progress over a number of years, teach us about pastoral care issues?
- What is meant by technical terms such as enrichment, extension, acceleration, multiple intelligences, compacting, mentoring, differentiation?
- How large should the target group be? (i.e. How many children are we going to regard as being able and talented?)
- Are there common characteristics for pupils generally able or for those talented in a specific area?
- How do we assess the work of able pupils?

Many of the questions above underpin sections of this book and the reader will find help on later pages. However more in-depth consideration of theoretical issues can be found in the suggested texts listed on pages 98-99.

Examples from recent 'official' texts which provide valuable guidance and information

1 'The Education of Very Able Children in Maintained Schools' *HMI Review 1992, (HMSO)*

HMI identified a number of factors associated with high standards of work. Most of them were directly linked to the quality of teaching and learning:

> - *close attention to the needs of the individual pupil through differentiation of tasks*
> - *careful monitoring of individual progress*
> - *teachers with a deep understanding of their subjects*
> - *high expectations of what pupils can achieve*
> - *appropriate choice of resources*
> - *pupils being encouraged to think for themselves, to ask questions, to take some responsibility for their own learning and to contribute ideas*
> - *variations in pace, teaching style and classroom organisation*
> - *a stimulating learning environment*

2 The National Curriculum

The HMI Review, above, suggested that the National Curriculum would assist the...

> *growing interest in differentiation in order to provide more appropriate levels of work for pupils across the whole ability range ....The National Curriculum is an important factor in this respect since it aims to raise achievement and highlights the need for schools to match work more closely to pupils' abilities.*

In the National Curriculum each subject order is prefaced by an enabling statement on ACCESS which includes the following:

> *The programme of study for each key stage should be taught to the great majority of pupils in the key stage, in ways appropriate to their abilities.*
>
> *For the small number of pupils who may need the provision, material may be selected from earlier or later key stages where this is necessary to enable individual pupils to progress and demonstrate achievement. Such material should be presented in contexts suitable to the pupil's age.*

'The National Curriculum', *Department for Education, (HMSO, 1995)*

Within the Level Descriptions there is the notion that...

> *By the end of Key Stage 3, the performance of the great majority of pupils should be within the range of Levels 2 to 6. Levels 7 and 8 are available for very able pupils and, to help teachers differentiate exceptional performance at Key Stage 3, a description above Level 8 is provided.*

It is worthwhile for departments to look at the Exceptional Performance paragraphs. They should provide valuable clues to what is required. If staff do not believe the paragraphs are clear enough or feel that they do not fully define exceptional performance, this is a good professional development opportunity for them to add their own statements, which would be helpful in planning the curriculum.

There have been many worries about some of the effects of the National Curriculum: the many, and frequent, changes have put considerable pressure on teachers: too much paperwork has damaged the time given to lesson planning and individual contact with pupils; the high emphasis on content may well have stifled other aspects of classroom management; and many teachers felt that the opportunity to use varied and more individual materials had been limited.

But even in its early stages the National Curriculum provided encouragement as well as causes for concern. It ensured a broad and balanced programme for all pupils, including the most able. There has been widespread appreciation of Sir Ron Dearing's slimming-down of both the content and the assessment procedures. The time thus 'freed' does assist the provision of enrichment and extension activities.

It is now important that teachers use the National Curriculum to the best advantage of more able pupils. Looking through the various subject orders one can find many sections which sit easily in a curriculum involving enrichment and extension and include the higher order skills. A small selection follows:

> *"...ask questions including 'what would happen if?' and 'why?', e.g. considering the behaviour of a programmable toy."* **(KS1, AT1, Mathematics)**

> *"...develop their own mathematical strategies and look for ways to overcome difficulties."* **(KS2, AT1, Mathematics)**

> *"...recognise that inferences drawn from data analysis of an experiment or enquiry may suggest further questions for investigations."* **(KS3 and 4, AT4, Mathematics)**

> *"...extend their mathematical reasoning into understanding and using more rigorous argument, leading to notions of proof."* **(KS4 Mathematics Further Material)**

> *"...to make predictions where it is appropriate to do so."* **(KS3, AT1, Science)**

> *"...to consider anomalies in observations or measurements and explain them where possible."* **(KS3, AT1, Science)**

> *"...analyse and discuss alternative interpretations, unfamiliar vocabulary, ambiguity and hidden meanings."* **(KS3 and 4, English)**

> *"...pupils should be given opportunities to talk for a range of purposes, including: planning, predicting and investigating, sharing ideas, insights and opinions."* **(KS2, AT1, English)**

> *"...prioritise and reconcile decisions on materials and components, production, time and costs within design proposals."* **(KS3, Design and Technology)**

> *"...develop a clear idea of what has to be done, proposing a sequence of actions, and suggesting alternative methods of proceeding if things go wrong."* **(KS2, Design and Technology)**

> *"...develop the ability to recognise patterns."* (KS2, Geography)
>
> *"...to analyse the characteristic features of particular periods and societies, including the range of ideas, beliefs and attitudes of people, and the experiences of men and women; and to analyse the social, cultural, religious and ethnic diversity of the societies studied."* (KS3, History)
>
> *"...to use increasingly advanced strategies and tactics of competitive play, and adapt these to the strengths and limitations of other players."* (KS4, Physical Education)
>
> *"...to develop their appreciation of the richness of our diverse cultural heritage."* (KS1,2 and 3, Music and Art)
>
> *"...learn by heart phrases and short extracts e.g. rhymes, poems, songs, jokes and tongue twisters."* (KS3 and 4, Modern Foreign Languages)

'The National Curriculum', *Department for Education, (HMSO, 1995)*

3 'OFSTED - A review of inspection findings 1993/4' *(HMSO, 1995)*

In reading the twelve booklets contained within this report, a number of relevant factors can be identified for consideration when designing a curriculum for the more able:

- constructive criticism
- high expectations
- open-ended tasks
- avoiding pupils being restricted by tightly prescribed tasks
- opportunities to experiment and to use initiative
- challenging aims shared with the pupils through clear instructions
- encouraging continuous review and evaluation
- more extended or creative written tasks
- an understanding of change and causation
- writing in response to investigation
- appropriate interactions with the teacher
- reference to the previous attainments of pupils
- relevant use of clubs, competitions and national contests
- developing higher order skills such as those of prediction and hypothesis
- ensuring pupils have the necessary understanding to plan their own practical work
- avoidance of over-directed teaching
- real pace
- continuity as pupils change from one phase to another
- where modules are used, proper progression from one to another
- pupils taking responsibility for their own learning
- adequate reflection
- pupils relating ideas to their own experience
- encouraging pupils to explore, select, practise and consolidate actions to improve performance
- accessing appropriate sources
- pupils stimulated to operate at the highest technical and analytic levels of which they are individually capable
- a purposeful development of knowledge and skills

The points are taken from specific subject booklets but collectively they provide a general catalogue of 'ingredients' for a curriculum for effective provision.

Procedures

Theory by itself achieves nothing. Practice, the effective provision for able and talented children, is what matters. The conversion of theory into good practice can only take place through the use of appropriate procedures, understood and followed by all members of the school community.

What do we need to do?

There are a number of essential steps which need to be taken towards creating effective provision for the able and talented in our schools. Each of the steps in the list below is fully explored within later sections of this book.

1. Establish a whole school policy. (Section Two)
2. Establish departmental policies. (Section Two)
3. Identify able and talented pupils through a variety of approaches including teacher referral, parental nomination, peer nomination, checklists and tests. (Sections Two and Three)
4. Use appropriate grouping strategies. (Section Six)
5. Set up a register of able and talented pupils. (Section Five)
6. Create Individual Education Plans. (Section Six)
7. Make human, financial and material resources available. (Sections Five and Nine)
8. Establish a monitoring and evaluation programme. (Section Eight)

Practice

It is important to remember that actions speak louder than words. What matters in the final analysis is that we make effective provision for children of all abilities. Understanding the relevant theory and taking note of the research enables appropriate policies to be formulated. However, theories have to be converted into practice by procedures. Without practical application what goes before becomes rather meaningless. Monitoring and evaluation point to ways in which practice could be improved.

KEY MESSAGE
Theory and practice must not be separated but rather should complement each other. The teacher needs to transfer the lessons learned elsewhere to inform the process of effective provision for able and talented children.

An everyday example to illustrate a central message of this book

The following example illustrates, by means of an analogy, how individuals can accomplish challenging goals within an institution that caters for groups with widely differing abilities and needs.

The basic scenario

The author wished to take beneficial exercise on a regular basis, gaining a sense of achievement without inflicting damage on the body. Swimming seemed to answer the bill. The time chosen was 10.00am on Sunday morning when a lane of the main pool is sectioned off for swimmers wanting to do lengths seriously. The target was to achieve forty lengths in thirty minutes. This was eventually achieved, although the target was

not attained until short breaks were included at the end of every ten lengths. This theoretically wasted time, but ultimately made success possible.

There are a number of ideas within this scenario that can be applied in a practical way to a school situation and which are particularly relevant to the issue of effective provision for able and talented pupils:

Local swimming pool	Practical application in school
During the week many groups of all ages and abilities are accommodated within the learner pool, the main pool and the continuous swimming lane. The groups, whether expert, handicapped or just seeking fun, can all gain benefit without conflicting with each other.	This example of excellent multi-purpose use of the one facility is an inspiration to grouping policy in schools to allow pupils of varying abilities, including the most able to receive effective provision.
To make the heart and lungs work hard at least twenty minutes' strong effort is required.	Pace and urgency, achieved through a demanding and challenging target, are beneficial features of attainment for at least some of the time.
The author masters sufficient technique to swim well but the style is far from perfect.	Theory must underlie the activity but there is scope for individuality and personal approach.
Even in the cordoned-off lane where the strong swimmers exercise there are marked differences in pace.	Even in the top set it will be necessary to accommodate significant differences of performance.
During the session there is a regular group of participants who are helped by a shared purpose, a group identity and the performance of others.	Able children need at least some contact with others of the same mind. This has implications for the organisation within the school.
It takes great willpower to get up and swim some Sunday mornings.	You need determination as well as ability to succeed.
The author does not keep increasing the target, which would be discouraging. He allows a little 'slippage' from time to time.	Try to avoid able pupils getting trapped on an A-grade treadmill which eventually becomes soul destroying.
The target was not achieved until rests were taken every ten lengths.	Breaking a task into manageable chunks ultimately enhances performance.

Meeting the needs of able pupils

Appropriate procedures convert good theory into effective provision which answers the needs of able pupils. This provision includes:

1. Question and answer sessions which promote the higher order thinking skills
2. Pastoral care alongside academic considerations
3. Independence of study, without losing contact with teachers
4. Enough space for trial and error and also for failure
5. A wide range of opportunities
6. Provision for the child's own benefit – not to please others
7. Contact for at least part of the time with children and/or adults of like mind and with similar interests
8. Various forms of differentiation: pace, outcome, support, dialogue, resource, task
9. A challenging but supportive environment
10. The correct starting point for the individual child
11. Opportunities to be creative and to use the imagination
12. Moving on when a skill or concept has been mastered
13. Pace and urgency
14. Tasks which allow individuality of response
15. A school ethos which promotes achievement and protects the achievers
16. A good balance of concrete and abstract tasks

In conclusion

- We need to acquire sufficient theory and evidence or our practice will be built upon poor foundations.

- Theory is only the starting point as policy documents and texts do not in themselves help able children.

- Procedures are the tools by which we get things done but they have to be followed by everybody.

- We should not separate education from real life as there are lessons all around us.

- The needs of able pupils have to be understood so that they will be served genuinely by the policies and practices undertaken by the school.

Section Two

Policy and beyond

In this section you will learn that:

➡ it is necessary to have a whole school policy in order to create an effective and consistent programme for staff to follow

➡ help in creating a policy is available from a number of sources

➡ there are key areas which must be included in a policy for effective provision, such as identification, in-class provision and grouping policy

➡ departmental policies are the next vital step in a whole school approach

➡ a school policy is the start, not the end of delivering effective provision

➡ the policy sets the scene for the programme

Why is a policy for able and talented pupils needed?

- Without a policy there will be little chance of consistency of approach; all members of the school need to be 'pulling in the same direction'. A policy does not guarantee consistency but it certainly helps to promote a shared purpose.
- Teachers need to have a point of reference so that they can check what should happen in particular circumstances.
- The education of able pupils now has a higher profile than in previous times (see Introduction). It is therefore sensible to give proper consideration to the issues involved.
- New members of staff, those who are on temporary contracts and student-teachers all need a policy document to which they can refer.
- Parents have a right to know what the school proposes to do. A written policy is the most sensible response.
- Able pupils themselves should have the facility to consult a document that outlines the school's approach to their teaching.
- A policy on able and talented pupils is needed to sit alongside other policies such as those on equal opportunities and gender issues.
- A successful policy on able and talented pupils will play a role in extending good practice to other pupils in the school.

KEY MESSAGE
The most important reason for a policy is that the chances of effective provision are greatly enhanced – the welfare of children should be at the heart of all our thinking.

How can you gather information?

For those schools without a policy, or for those with a policy but who would like to compare their own approach with other examples, here are some possible routes.

1. Ask the Local Education Authority if your school can see the area policy, if there is one. Alternatively, ask to see the policies of other schools who do not mind sharing their work. Some schools make their policy available commercially.

2. If you are a member of a national association such as NACE – the National Association for Able Children in Education – you can ask to inspect the bank of examples kept at their central office.

3. Share ideas with a group of neighbouring schools.

4. Read the relevant sections in published texts. Each of the following texts has appropriate content:

'School Governors and More Able Children', *Deborah Eyre, (NACE/DfEE 1995)*

'Gifted Education: Identification and Provision', *David George (David Fulton 1995)*

'A School Policy on Provision for Able Pupils', *J B Teare (NACE/DfEE, 2nd edition 1996)*

What should a school policy cover?

Here are some examples of elements to consider in formulating policies.

1. In 'School Governors and More Able Children', Deborah Eyre suggests that...

This should include both the school's philosophical approach and the practical mechanisms which convert policy to practice.

She goes on to list sections on:

- General rationale
- Aims
- Definitions
- General overall approach
- Identification and monitoring schemes
- Organisational responses
- In class approach
- Out of class activities
- Personal and social education
- Responsibility for co-ordinating and monitoring progress
- Process for review and development
- Use of outside agencies for training, provision, etc.

2. In 'Gifted Education: Identification and Provision', David George suggests in his chapter on Policies, that the following items might form the basis of such a document:

- Consistent terminology and definition
- Senior Management defining and agreeing methods for screening, registering and monitoring the progress of pupils with these abilities
- Advice on identifying gifted and talented children

- Aims and objectives which reflect the idea that provision for able children should be seen as an aspect of provision for all pupils
- A sense of ownership by the staff
- Teachers providing opportunities for pupils to practise and develop their particular abilities
- A directory of useful local expertise
- A grouping policy of working with peers for social and emotional maturity.
- A collection of appropriate differentiated responses
- Records, monitoring children's progress

Here is a more detailed exploration of points to be included in a policy. Explanations of many of these points will follow in later sections of this book.

1) Introduction	a) The need for a whole school policy
	b) Departmental statements
	c) A consistent approach
	d) A policy for action, not lying on the bookshelf
2) General approach	a) The school's firm intention
	b) Seeing able pupils as an opportunity not a problem
	c) Welcoming the challenge
	d) Striving for excellence
3) Who are the most able?	a) Inclusive approach not an exclusive system
	b) Provision for the truly outstanding
	c) Inclusion of a fair proportion of the school population
	d) Looking at wide and differing areas of ability
	e) Confronting the issue of able underachievers
	f) Looking to involve able pupils with handicaps
	g) An underachievers referral sheet
4) Identification	a) Trying to keep an open mind
	b) Use of a pupil referral sheet
	c) A register of able and talented pupils
	d) Letter to encourage parental nomination
	e) Use of general checklists
	f) Use of subject checklists
	g) Positive use of tests
	h) Inservice work to aid teachers in identifying able and talented pupils
	i) Peer nomination
	j) Record-keeping systems to provide further questions
5) Grouping policy	a) The unsuitability of streaming
	b) Setting, but within rules
	c) Mixed ability, where the able are challenged
	d) Working with older pupils
6) Curriculum	a) Establishing appropriate curriculum principles
	b) Work schemes promoting differentiation of various types
	c) The use of enrichment activities
	d) Differentiated homeworks
	e) A range of strategies both within and outside the school
	f) The use of Individual Education Plans

7) Assessment	a) A longitudinal view of ability
	b) The concept of value added
	c) Pupil evidence
	d) Monitoring and evaluation to inform future planning
	e) Flexible assessment to take account of the unusual response
	f) Signposts to ability and false signals
8) Pastoral care	a) Concern for the whole person
	b) Peer pressure problems
	c) Accommodation of the individual within the institution
	d) Rewards and sanctions
9) Parents	a) Working co-operatively
	b) Recognising, and then preventing, possible conflict
	c) Sharing information
10) Other phases	a) Getting information from the previous stage
	b) Handing on information to the next stage
	c) Running joint activities
11) Organisation	a) The role of the Co-ordinator for Able and Talented pupils
	b) Links with the Senior Management Team
	c) The place of able and talented pupils within the Special Needs work of the school
	d) The part to be played by the governing body
12) Inservice	a) The present deficiencies in training
	b) Provision of suitable Inservice
	c) Promoting positive teacher attitudes
	d) A range of strategies to assist the classroom teacher
13) Conclusion	A quickfire list of key points

Beyond the policy

The policy is a starting point only; it has to be put into operation effectively. Monitoring and evaluation are needed to identify weak links and to make improvements. It is also vital that the Able and Talented Co-ordinator (see Section Five: Personnel) keeps abreast of national developments – there have been many changes in recent years and the same movement is likely to continue.

We are aiming at a moving target!

Departmental policies

Following the agreement of a whole school policy there needs to be the development of departmental policies in secondary schools and curriculum area policies in primary schools. What should they cover? Here are some suggestions:

1. A rationale for the document
2. A discussion on who constitutes the target group
3. Thoughts on what constitutes ability in the particular curriculum area
4. How responsibility for able and talented pupils is to be covered in the department
5. The use and possible modification of whole school procedures
6. Identification strategies
7. The writing of the department's own Exceptional Performance Paragraph to sit alongside the one in the National Curriculum document
8. The creation of a subject checklist of the characteristics of able pupils in the curriculum area
9. Strategies for classroom provision
10. Strategies for additional activities – competitions, mentors, use of outside agencies etc.
11. How the assessment policy takes note of able pupils
12. Pastoral concerns (these will vary – look at the Physical Education example on p.45
13. The present suitability of resources and how they might be extended
14. The Inservice requirements of the teachers in the department, depending on past experience and training
15. How the effectiveness of the department's work will be monitored and evaluated

The policy as an agenda setter

The policy creates the blueprint for the work ahead. It gives direction to the short-term and middle-term action plans. In the longer term the policy itself may need review and revision.

In conclusion

- A whole school policy is a vital part of the process and this should involve all members of the school community.

- This policy needs to be monitored and regularly updated to keep abreast of developments.

- Departmental policies should sit within the whole school policy but should permit 'acceptable diversity' to accommodate the needs of the differing curriculum areas.

- A policy document is not there to gather dust on the bookcase but rather to act as a blueprint for action.

Section Three

Identification

> **This section will consider:**
>
> ➡ the size of the target group
>
> ➡ which children might be regarded as able and talented
>
> ➡ some of the difficulties involved in identification
>
> ➡ the main methods used in identification
>
> ➡ procedures to help the collection of data

How many children are we talking about?

There is a clinical definition of the term 'gifted' accepted by a number of people in the field. It is:

> **Those who are more than two standards of deviation from the mean on a normal distribution curve of intelligence.**

Standard deviations from different tests vary. They can be 15 or 20, thus giving a measure of 130+ or 140+. Looking at the normal distribution curve of intelligence in this way gives 2% in the target group. Some providers would be more selective and would go for more than three standard deviations. Many programmes in the United States would look to narrow down the group to a fraction of 1%. There is an American phrase which refers to the 'severely gifted'!

Schools often prefer to think in terms of a percentage figure. Many have settled for a target group of 10%. But there are problems with defining a target group in this type of way as the boundaries soon become blurred. If you start with a nominal 10% of pupils for example, the figure will expand as you move into more and more areas of the curriculum. Very few children are able 'across the board'. Nomination lists from teachers in specific activities or subjects will have some overlap, but only some. As an illustration, the 10% in the Department of Education in Science work carried out by Cliff Denton and Keith Postlethwaite in Oxfordshire some years ago, grew to above 20% when only four subjects were involved.

Schools do vary but this sort of approach may very well lead to 30% of the school population being considered in one or more areas.

KEY MESSAGE

We are talking about a considerable number of children. Identification should be inclusive rather than exclusive. We should be looking to expand the pool of talent.

Who are the able and talented?

It is important to consider what is meant by the term 'able and talented', and the sorts of pupils who might be included in the school's target group.

We are talking about exceptional children

Part of our work is to provide for the few truly outstanding children. Some years ago a young boy called Ganesh Sittampalam was featured in the colour supplement of **'The Mail on Sunday'**. The article started:

> *Ganesh Sittampalam was five when his parents realised that he might be more than ordinarily bright. He had just learned about fractions when one day he turned to his father and said, 'Daddy, if you take 1 and add 1/2 to it, and then add 1/4 and then 1/8 and so on, you get closer and closer to 2, but you never actually get there.'*
>
> *A few weeks later he said, 'Mummy, do you realise that if you take any number and square it, then add one to it and square that, the difference between those two squares is the sum of the two original numbers. If the numbers are two apart, the result is two times the sum. I wonder if it keeps going like that?'*

The article went on to chronicle the next years in Ganesh's remarkable development.

We are talking about many more children

Children such as Ganesh are exceptional and schools do not see too many pupils like him. However, the able and talented programme is also about a considerable number of other children who need to be identified and then provision made for them.

We are talking about a wide range of abilities

Of course, we are concerned with high intellectual ability, with those who score highly in IQ terms, with those who might be termed intelligent or clever or bright....BUT we are also concerned with:

- sporting ability
- musical talent
- dramatic talent
- innovative designers
- creativity
- leadership skills
- organisational ability
- mechanical ingenuity
- a high level of interpersonal skills
- any human ability or talent which has meaning for the individual and/or society

Those wishing to research this idea further would be well advised to look at Howard Gardner's book **'Frames of Mind'** *(Fontana Press, 2nd ed., 1993)*, in which he listed seven intelligences:

1. Linguistic
2. Musical
3. Logical – Mathematical
4. Spatial
5. Bodily – Kinesthetic
6. Intrapersonal
7. Interpersonal

Effective Provision for Able & Talented Children

Another list appears in **'The Empty Raincoat'** by Charles Handy *(Hutchinson, 1994)*

1. **Factual Intelligence**
2. **Analytical Intelligence**
3. **Linguistic Intelligence**
4. **Spatial Intelligence**
5. **Musical Intelligence**
6. **Practical Intelligence**
7. **Physical Intelligence**
8. **Intuitive Intelligence.**
9. **Interpersonal Intelligence**

KEY MESSAGE
Whichever model you want to use, do make your target group wide and varied. All human abilities and talents are to be cherished and nourished.

To test your understanding of the wide perspective of ability, try the following exercise:

1. Decide upon a model of abilities, talents or intelligences.
2. Name some famous people who fit the categories.
3. Explain why.
4. Now think of children you are teaching or have taught and find examples for each category.

We need to avoid stereotyping

There is a famous 'The Far Side' cartoon showing a child pushing strongly against a door labelled 'pull', trying to enter a building signposted as 'Midvale School for the Gifted'. The cartoon portrays one stereotype of the very able child – the absent-minded little professor who has enormous talents in an academic area but who lacks common sense and fails to fit in with the simple needs of looking after oneself. There are such people but they are few in number.

What we can say is that able and talented children come in every shape, size, nationality and character. There are no set rules and therefore there are no foolproof routes to identification.

KEY MESSAGE
We need to keep an open mind as to who are the able and talented.

Ability is not always easy to spot

Researchers differ about how accurate teachers are in identifying the able and talented. What we do know is that many people have 'escaped the net'. It is a salutary lesson to be reminded that we don't always get it right. A few examples illustrate the point:

1. The psychologists, Illingworth and Illingworth, made a study of the childhood of 450 famous men and women. Many had been well regarded by their parents and teachers but an extensive list of those who were not regarded as able, formed the basis of a chapter entitled 'Unrecognised Ability'. A couple of examples give the flavour. Leo

Tolstoy was described as *"both unable and unwilling to learn"*. Louis Pasteur was only a mediocre pupil in his Baccalaureate.

2. A local East Devon newspaper, **'Pulman's Weekly News'** in 1990 wrote about a 15 year-old boy, Kristian Maess, who had failed examinations at 11 and 13 to get into grammar school yet who had been admitted to Mensa on a staggering IQ score of 174. Mensa executive Harold Gale commented, *"It puts him in the top 1% for intelligence in the country"*.

3. Roald Dahl's English Composition report when aged 16 said, *"This boy is an indolent and illiterate member of the class"* (from the book **'The Wonderful Story of Henry Sugar and Six More'**, *(Puffin Books, 1995)*

4. 'They said I was useless, but look at me now' was the title of an article by Anne Nicholls in the education section of **'The Independent'** in January 1993. She interviewed four people with particular stories to tell. One was Barney Edwards, one of Britain's leading directors of television commercials. He had an unspectacular education (his Maths teacher called him MD for mentally deficient) and a disastrous spell at art college. About going to London, Barney Edwards said:

> *Despite my lack of academic success, I learnt three very important things: to take responsibility for my actions, to communicate well and to think both analytically and creatively......Few schools today teach you to think. Now, when I employ someone I don't care whether they have been to university or if they have any qualifications. I want to know what films they see, what books they read, whether they have courage, charisma, stamina and can really communicate.*

5. Talent can sometimes only be discovered by accident or unusual circumstances. A particularly good example is that of Dame Alicia Markova. In **'Markova Remembers'** *(Hamish Hamilton, 1986)* she says:

> *I was a docile, even-tempered child, curious about life but silent, solemn-eyed and very frail. Because of childhood ill-health, my education was intermittent, and dancing lessons were begun in order to strengthen what were thought to be weak limbs. My little flat footprints were noted in the sands at Bognor, where we were on holiday, and our doctor suggested that the exercise of classical ballet would strengthen my legs and feet.*

But for this opportunity a great talent would never have been revealed.

KEY MESSAGES
- Ability is longitudinal – things change. People develop at different rates, therefore you cannot take too much notice of a single measure at a particular point in time.

- Some people confound the expectations of their parents and teachers. Children seen early in life as 'clever' turn out to be superficially bright. The talents of others are not spotted even by those close to them. Thus lack of early recognition is not conclusive.

- So-called weaknesses can turn out to be towers of strength. Coping with problems can ultimately enhance your capabilities. There is a well-known story about Michelangelo producing his masterpiece 'David' from a block of marble damaged by another sculptor. It was the damage itself which provided Michelangelo with the key to how the sculpture should be made.

- Achievement comes through many routes, sometimes roundabout ways.

- Talent is multi-faceted and therefore we need a broad approach to recognise all its facets. Much talent remains undiscovered and unused unless the correct opportunity comes along. Indeed, some people's abilities are only discovered by accident. (How many more sets of flat footprints have been left in the sand and not been noticed...?)

How do teachers identify able and talented pupils?

There are various 'tools' which can be used in the identification process of able and talented children, e.g. – checklists, ability tests, end-of-module tests, parental nominations. Let's look at the merits and limitations of these in turn.

1 General checklists

A general checklist should include a group of characteristics which help to identify an able or talented child. If a particular pupil matches a good proportion of the qualities described, this is taken as evidence pointing towards high ability.

As well as the author's own points, the following general checklist incorporates suggestions from the following: **'Primary Guidelines for Gifted and More Able Children'** *(written by REACH for Solihull Metropolitan Borough Council Education Department)*; SR Laycock's list in **'Gifted Children and their Education'**, *Hoyle and Wilks (Des, 1974)*; **'Educating the Able'**, *D Montgomery (Cassell, 1996)*; **'Teaching the Very Able Child'**, *B Wallace (Ward Lock Educational Ltd., 1983)*; **'Helping the Child of Exceptional Ability'**, *S Leyden (Croom Helm, 1985)*; **'Foundations for NAGC Leaders'**, *(NAGC)*.

1. Possesses superior powers of reasoning, of dealing with abstractions, of generalising from specific facts, of understanding meanings, and of seeing into relationships. *(Laycock)*

2. Originality and initiative in intellectual and practical work. *(Montgomery)*

3. Information can be absorbed quickly and stored, sifted, analysed and organised to develop coherent and complex arguments. *(NAGC)*

4. Has a devastating appreciation of the weaknesses of other people including those in positions of authority such as teachers. *(Teare)*

5. Unusually high personal standards; frustration if they cannot achieve the excellence they demand of themselves; perfectionist approach, not satisfied with approval from others. *(Leyden)*

6. When interested becomes absorbed for long periods and may be impatient with interference or abrupt change. *(Wallace)*

7. Keen powers of observation, noting mismatches and analogies. *(Montgomery)*

8. Adapts articles readily and uses them for purposes other than those for which they were intended. *(Teare)*

9. Constant repetition of skills already fluent will usually lead to loss of interest. *(NAGC)*

10. Preference for the company of older children and adults; boredom with the company and interests of peers. *(Leyden)*

11. Has exceptional curiosity and constantly wants to know why. *(Wallace)*

12. Has great interest in the nature of man and the universe (problems of origins and destiny, etc.). *(Laycock)*

13. Has ability to lead and influence others – this may show in positive or negative behaviour. *(Solihull)*

14. Spots the direction of a story or situation well ahead of peers. *(Teare)*

15. Pursues subjects or a subject in great depth. *(Montgomery)*

16. Unwilling to follow instructions for class tasks; preferring to do things in an individual manner. *(Solihull)*

17. Wide range of interests: hobbies that are sometimes unusual and which are followed with great enthusiasm and competence. Often keen collectors. *(Leyden)*

18. Sees connections, relationships, inconsistencies, cause and effect, bias, and the distinction between fact and opinion in the manner of the average child at least half as old again. *(NAGC)*

KEY MESSAGES

- One, or even a small number of matches with characteristics in a checklist does not provide strong evidence of ability – e.g. being unwilling to follow instructions for class tasks could be a sign of lack of concentration in a child of <u>low</u> ability.

- A high match of characteristics may be indicative of high ability – but this depends upon the quality of the checklist.

- An able child may display opposite characteristics to individual items in the checklist, even though there is correlation on other points – e.g. an able child might have a butterfly mind and therefore not become absorbed in particular activities.

- Checklists are an aid to identification but they should not be used inflexibly or independently of other methods of identification as we then run the risk of creating stereotypes – and we know that children can be very different.

2 Subject checklists

General checklists do have a place and a use but subject checklists have greater practical value. The principles behind the general checklist still operate but now the characteristics reflect high ability in a particular curriculum area.

Below is a possible plan of action for compiling a checklist for Mathematics. The same procedures could also be used for other subjects.

1. Brainstorm characteristics in a departmental meeting.

2. As part of an Inservice session define carefully what you mean by high mathematical ability.

3. Use actual pieces of work from pupils as discussion points.

4. Draw upon any case studies that you have, either from your own school or elsewhere.

5. Research work done already by experts in the field – for example:

a) VA Krutetskii,'**The Psychology of Mathematical Abilities in Schoolchildren'** (*University of Chicago Press, 1976*) is regarded as a wonderful source by many mathematicians. According to Krutetskii, there are three basic stages of mental activity in solving a mathematical problem: gathering the information needed to solve the problem, processing the information so as to obtain a solution, and retaining information about the solution.

b) As part of the Schools Council Programme 4, Anita Straker wrote **'Mathematics for Gifted Pupils'**, (*Longmans, 1983*). She listed characteristics for pre-school or infant children including:

- a liking for numbers including use of them in stories and rhymes
- precision in positioning toys

For older children she went on to look for other identifiers including:

- persistence in a search for the best and simplest solution to a problem
- terse sentences and a pronounced use of number within pieces of writing

c) Roy Kennard's **'Teaching Mathematically Able Children'**, (*NACE/DfEE, 1996)*, has been well received. The book starts with 'Perspectives on the characteristic mathematical abilities of able children'.

d) The policy documents of advisory staff or other schools.

Below are two examples of subject checklists to help in the identification of ability in particular areas.

Music

For an exhibition of materials on the teaching and learning of able pupils in September 1996, Devon Youth Music prepared a leaflet on Musically Able Pupils. This included the following subject checklist:

Able music students may demonstrate any or all of the following:

- *perform exceptionally well on a solo instrument*
- *show great sensitivity in group performance*
- *sing with unusual quality and style*
- *compose original music with flair and invention*
- *redraft compositions with uncommon speed and accuracy*
- *display excellent oral skills*
- *learn and understand technical aspects of music extremely quickly*
- *show exceptional understanding of culture and historical styles*

History

A child with a particular ability in History:

- Enjoys accumulating knowledge by reading and research
- Has a healthy scepticism about evidence and sources, and therefore has an appreciation of the limitations of the conclusions reached
- Is sensitive to the weighting of various pieces of evidence
- Possesses a strong sense of chronology and development
- Has an ability to divorce his or her self from the present with its assumptions and contexts
- Has the intellectual capacity to understand complex theories and concepts
- Has the capacity to 'get inside' lives and events at previous times and in other places
- Appreciates the complexity behind human actions thus taking due consideration of a variety of causes
- Has the ability to impose a pattern of thought across a wide spectrum of information and sources

For written work there are some other important abilities which will lead to examination success:

- Has good reading and study skills which allow the extraction of key data quickly
- Possesses advanced language skills which leads to good expression of thoughts, including the choice of the appropriate word or phrase that really gets to the heart of the idea to be conveyed
- Has the ability to organise thoughts into a logical sequence which enhances the reader's understanding of the concepts involved
- Displays subtlety and finesse in the presentation of material including the use of pertinent quotations and the interesting juxtapositioning of ideas

KEY MESSAGES

- Subject checklists tend to be of greater practical value than general checklists because the judgements are made as a more normal part of the teacher's work, especially in relation to schemes of work and assessment. Also, the subject characteristics, being more specific, are easier to identify.

- The compilation of subject checklists is a valuable part of Inservice work as teachers have to analyse the curriculum area and decide what it is that indicates high ability. This process assists other thinking on effective provision, linking the needs of able pupils to the 'nuts and bolts' of the subject and to what constitutes quality answers. The thinking behind subject checklists thus helps teachers to identify, to assess children's work, and to make effective provision.

3 Testing

This subject could fill a book. Space necessitates comments being limited.

DO:
- Add test scores to all the identification information which is available
- Use scores positively, i.e. take note when a child scores highly, especially where ability is not well regarded
- Look favourably upon the establishment of a regular procedure to run, for example, NFER Cognitive Abilities Tests
- Make sure that tests are administered meticulously in accordance with the instructions from the authors
- Recognise that tests have margins of error

DO N'T:
- Put over-emphasis on test results
- Extrapolate results into areas outside the competence of the test
- Ignore results provided by parents or by outside agencies, but rather try to merge their significance into wider data
- Allow tests to over-dominate the curriculum so that time is not available for interesting and challenging tasks
- Be 'steamrollered' by statistical evidence without placing it in a correct context. Numbers can take on a magic of their own

There is a danger that tests and examinations become dominated by methods which seem to offer easy measurements. Life does not tend to be that simple. A cartoon by Bill Stott showed a past Prime Minister and Secretary for Education watching a child being prepared to be dipped into a tank of 'Formula X'; the caption read, *"There! The simple test you've been looking for – just dip the kid in and if he turns blue, it's a pass."*

It is also worth bearing in mind this quote, taken from a US report entitled **'Education Counts'**:

> *We must learn to measure what we value rather than valuing what we can easily measure.*

To illustrate some of the dangers of testing, here are two instances where correct, but unexpected, answers can easily be discounted:

Multiple choice questions

There is concern that able and talented children may not mark the expected response because:
  a) the answer is 'too easy' and they ignore it, thinking there must be a catch
  b) they see a correct answer through a much more convoluted route, as in the example below

Which of the following is the odd one out?
stable   tractor   tent   house   cave

The expected answer (for one mark) is tractor, as the others are homes of one sort or another.

The alternative answer (scoring no mark) is house, as it is the only word which does not take the prefix con- (constable; contractor; content; concave).

The result is that able pupils receive less credit than those of lower ability because they think too deeply. Good assessment is about finding what candidates know, not misleading them.

Questions requiring memorised or rigid answers
In a physics examination candidates were expected to repeat a learnt specific example which illustrated a principle. An able pupil could not remember the exact example but understood the principle so well that he made up an equally good example during the examination. This caused a dispute as his alternative answer was not credited.

KEY MESSAGE
Unless the marking scheme and instructions for tests and examinations are carefully thought out, outstanding responses might receive no credit.

4 Nomination
Another important method of identification is nomination – not only by teachers, but also by parents and peers.

● Teacher nomination
Before nominating a child as able and talented teachers will have used one or more of the identification 'tools' described above. Teachers need to be encouraged and helped to nominate able and talented pupils. A suitable Inservice provision helps to sensitise teachers so that they are more capable of identifying and providing for able and talented children (see Section Five: Personnel). A document, such as the following, is needed.

Able and talented pupils - referral sheet

Name of Pupil:

Form:

Teacher making referral:

Please indicate the area(s) of ability/talent

What are the sources of evidence on which the referral is made? (E.g. Observation, test results, subject or general checklist, internal examination, homework, classwork, parental nomination)

What recommendations, if any, would you make on an Individual Education Plan?

Signed:

Date:

There are various ways of setting out such a referral sheet. What is important is that the form is user-friendly. Many professions are swamped by paperwork and there is a danger that an initial document is not completed for fear of the weight of paper and enormous consumption of time which follows. The sheet shown is designed to be simple to complete and therefore is more likely to be used. This initial step does not need too much detail as the Able and Talented Co-ordinator (See Section Five) can discuss its contents with the member of staff who filled it in.

●   <u>Parental nomination</u>

Parents should be consulted as part of the identification process. They have a unique perspective which adds to the total picture of a pupil. Involving parents increases the likelihood of cooperation between school and home, which is in the best interests of the child. However, encouraging parental nomination can bring potential conflicts:

- The staff may be concerned that parents take an exaggerated view of a child's ability and the inflated opinion then produces a situation in which the school can't win.
- Parents may believe that the school only wants children nominated who have truly outstanding ability.

The first step towards parental nomination is a general letter, such as the one that follows:

Dear Parents,

ABLE AND TALENTED PUPILS

By law, schools have to draw up a register of pupils with Special Educational Needs and then to take steps in a prescribed order as outlined in the Code of Practice. This school also wishes to draw up a register of pupils who are particularly able in one or more activity or curriculum area. This ability could be in a subject area within the classroom or it could be in an activity outside the school. The register would help to ensure that students' activities were being catered for in a variety of ways.

This letter is an invitation for you to write to me with information. Much of what you say will already be known by members of staff. Such information will not be wasted as it will help confirm views held by the school. Other information may well be additional to what we already know and will therefore be particularly useful.

We are not looking just for nominations of truly outstanding pupils. Research would indicate that perhaps in excess of 30% of the children in this school could justifiably be nominated in one area or another – especially when we consider all human talents and abilities.

There are some problems associated with this process. Many parents, not surprisingly, look very favourably upon their children and this may lead to a falsely high opinion of ability. Another factor which could inflate an estimate of ability is that parents do not have the same opportunities to compare a large number of children, unlike teachers. Despite these potential problems, I still believe it is sensible to ask your views. Parents spend more time with their children than do teachers and they see them in different circumstances. As a consequence they are sometimes aware of talents and abilities which have not been spotted elsewhere.

If you believe that your child does have a particular talent or possesses high ability could you please write to me, naming the area(s) of ability and explain why you think this to be the case.

Yours sincerely,

In the author's experience parents do not go 'over the top' in their replies but tend rather to be modest about their children. They sometimes have a different perspective of a particular ability, which is very helpful in the information-gathering process. It is also worth noting that parents value this opportunity.

KEY MESSAGES
- Parental nomination is a valuable process
- The advantages far outweigh the potential dangers
- The parent body welcomes such an opportunity

- **Peer nomination**

If we are looking to seek out as many worthwhile routes to identification as possible, it would be foolish to rule out peer nomination. Children have a different perception about who is able. They may well use an alternative set of criteria. They also see ability put to the test in contexts very different from the classroom.

One of the problems is how to get to that information without causing upset. Straight questions, in isolation, may not be appropriate. However, the relevant answers could be obtained within a more general questionnaire. Some schools for instance ask Year 7 pupils a number of questions about how they have found their first year at secondary school. Amongst questions on likes, dislikes, problems etc. could be questions asking the child what he or she is good at, as well as asking which children in their class have particular abilities and what those abilities are.

5 Provision

The best identifier of all is provision. Do you know, for example, whether you can throw a javelin well, or ice skate or paint Chinese style? Have you ever tried? Some people have great abilities without knowing they are there – and without the opportunity to try out latent talents, they will remain undiscovered.

How appropriate are traditional methods of identification?

Most traditional methods used to identify abilities and talents – such as testing and interviewing – have extreme limitations. Can we test for creativity, for example? There are tests – Torrance, Urban etc. – but how much can they tell us? Can we test for all human abilities and talents?

Consider this list from a leaflet by the Engineering Council called **'Engineering for People'**:

> *Engineering needs people with a range of talents:*
> - *Willingness to keep abreast of new technology*
> - *Flexibility to cope with changing demand*
> - *Entrepreneurial skills to develop new business*
> - *Ability to negotiate and compromise*
> - *A sense of humour*
> - *Willingness to take decisions on incomplete or conflicting data*
> - *Manual dexterity and the ability to make things*
> - *Adaptability to different climates and food and being away from home*
> - *Ability to take responsibility*
> - *Respect for our environment*

Which of these talents could you test for? Which identification strategies could be used for which talents? Grasp of new technology and manual dexterity could be assessed via practical tests; a sense of humour may come out in interview; respect for the environment might become evident from activities followed by the applicant. However, some of the talents would need considerable time to assess and might not be apparent (or otherwise) for months or years. The range is wide and the suitability of individuals would not be clear from many traditional forms of identification.

In conclusion

- We are talking about truly exceptional children but we are also looking at a range of talents and abilities which could involve 30-40% of the school population.

- Some able pupils are easy to spot, others are much more difficult to identify.

- General checklists aid teacher nomination provided that they do not create stereotypes.

- Subject checklists, tests, parental nomination, teacher referral, peer nomination and examinations all have a part to play in identification but each has weaknesses as well as strengths, so the more methods that can be used the better.

- Provision is not only the best identifier, it is also the reason for identification being carried out. To identify able children and then not provide for them is pointless.

Section Four

School ethos and pastoral care

In this section you will learn that:

➡ there is concern about some able pupils underachieving

➡ a supportive school ethos is very important

➡ many able children are well integrated but others face problems

➡ teacher attitudes can make a real difference

➡ planning should involve pastoral as well as curriculum considerations

➡ a productive partnership with parents is of great value

Underachievement

'Collins English Dictionary' defines underachievement as *"the failure to achieve a performance appropriate to one's age or talents"*. Clearly underachievement can occur at any level of ability including the highest.

A number of researchers and authors have attempted to list the characteristics of able underachievers.

A composite list of characteristics of able underachievers

- A marked difference between the quality of oral and written work
- A task started well but then unfinished and/or rushed as concentration diminishes
- Bored for much of the time but odd flashes of brilliance when interested
- A poor team member failing to co-operate in a group situation
- Hypercritical of the efforts of themselves and other people
- Often day-dreaming rather than getting on with the task in hand
- Performing noticeably better in just one or two areas where the relationship with the teacher 'gels'
- Shows a dislike of routine tasks but sometimes sparkles when the work is of a more unusual nature
- Wide mood swings, making it difficult for other people to get a reasonably consistent response
- Posing challenging questions showing perception but not always for positive reasons

Why does underachievement occur?

Some possible reasons may be:

<u>Peer Pressure</u>

In some schools it is not 'cool' to succeed. Able children can often incur the displeasure of their peers by doing well at school, especially in academic areas. This is particularly true when the child does not have the 'saving grace' of being good at sport and / or being the leading light socially. Being able at Physics for example may not commend the child to their friends but being the best shooter on the netball team or having great skill on a skateboard can soften the blow.

Consider this dialogue taken from a cartoon strip in **'Teacher's Weekly'** some years ago:

Teacher:	*"Very well done!"*
Teacher:	*"Excellent work."*
Teacher:	*"I really am very pleased."*

(Child shows clear signs of discomfort)
Teacher (perplexed): *"What's the matter – aren't you pleased?"*
Child (with considerable feeling): *"Yes Miss. But I've got to think of my playground credibility!"*

KEY MESSAGE

If we want our able pupils to perform to the correct level, schools have to make high achievement acceptable. This is difficult because of the prevailing social climate and the level of peer pressure. The school has to create an atmosphere in which success is valued by everybody. School ethos, a Code of Achievement and special displays are among the ideas discussed later in this section.

<u>Personality</u>

Some of the reasons for underachievement may well stem from the natural personality of the child. Section Three of this book, Identification, discussed the danger of creating stereotypes. It is worth repeating here that not all able children are hard-working, honest, teacher-pleasing, consciencious, socially at ease etc. An able pupil who is lazy will see no great point in working hard to produce the sort of results of which they are capable. An able pupil may very well have a 'butterfly mind' which flits from place to place without completion of a task. Intelligence, talent and creativity may not necessarily be supplemented by 'stickability' and therefore underachievement occurs, frustrating those who know the true potential.

<u>The social climate</u>

Some societies do not seem to value success. The British media are not always appreciative of ability. Newspapers prefer 'colourful characters' to people who succeed without causing scenes or insulting others.

<u>Gender</u>

There has been a long history of able girls not receiving the same attention as their male counterparts nor of having the same opportunities to progress. Ironically the educational world is now struggling with the issue of underachieving boys.

Family background

Able children from families where there is no history of academic excellence, perhaps also living in an area where books are not an accepted part of the landscape, face a number of problems. Support and advice might be in short supply. Lack of transport mobility can restrict the taking-up of opportunities. Older children being expected to look after their younger brothers and sisters may not find the time to complete homework or carry out research activities. Lack of material comforts will inhibit learning. The absence of study facilities will damage progress.

Handicaps

Able pupils with visual, hearing and physical problems are likely to underachieve. Those who are dyslexic are also going to encounter difficulties.

Note: Those wishing to explore the topic of underachievement would do well to read the excellent chapter 'Helping the underfunctioning able' in Diane Montgomery's book **'Educating the Able'**, *(Cassell, 1996)*.

Combatting underachievement

Gathering information is the first requirement. The school needs data on pupils whose attainment is less than their potential. Where possible, factors causing the problem need to be diagnosed and then, most important, professionals both inside the school and without need to plan remedial action. Below there is a copy of an Underachieving Pupil Referral Sheet which aims to collect the necessary information.

This sheet may provide explanations which fit the various causes of underachievement already noted. Confirmation from more than one teacher or area of the curriculum helps to identify the specific problems and possible ways forward.

Underachieving Pupil Referral Sheet

Name of Pupil:

Form:

Subject/ Area/ Activity:

Comment upon present level of performance

What is the potential performance?

What is the evidence for suggesting that the pupil can do better?

Why do you believe that there is underachievement?
(temporary or more permanent causes)

Have you any practical suggestions to help the performance level?

Teacher's Name:

Signature:

Date:

To combat peer pressure the school ethos has to create an atmosphere in which the able can achieve without receiving unfavourable attention from others. Below are five specific suggestions:

1 Stress to pupils that it is to be expected that individuals will progress at different rates. This theme has to be promoted in the Personal and Social Education Programme and in assemblies. Suitable quotes can be included, e.g.:

> *"We are not here to beat each other, but to pace each other on the road to perfection."*

Sir Walford Davies

2 Display catchphrases and key messages around the school, especially in recreational areas. The National Association for Able Children in Education produce two sets of posters to motivate pupils and teachers respectively. One from the pupil pack suggests:

> *"Success comes in cans, not in can'ts!"*

3 As well as running events specifically for able and talented pupils, promote more general enrichment activities which give opportunities to pupils of all abilities (see Section Seven).

4 Write, and display in each classroom, a Code of Achievement, such as the one below, and include that code in the tutorial programme.

CODE OF ACHIEVEMENT

"HAPPINESS LIES IN THE JOY OF ACHIEVEMENT AND THE THRILL OF CREATIVE EFFORT"
Franklin D. Roosevelt.

1) All areas of activity (sport, music, drama, community, leadership, charity, creativity, academic etc.) are regarded as of equal status.

2) Achievement in any area of activity is to be celebrated.

3) The school aims to promote achievement for pupils of all abilities to the level at which they individually can perform.

4) Recognising and celebrating the achievement of others is seen to be as important as striving for personal success.

5) The school aims to create an atmosphere in which there is encouragement and appreciation of success rather than envy.

---

5 Recognise, publicly, in assemblies or elsewhere, the achievements of all pupils across the full spectrum of school activities.

Other courses of action in dealing with pupils' underachievement

- With the help of other professionals, provide advice and support for those with personality and social problems.
- Analyse gender differences in performance and take action. As an example, Lynn Fox and Wendy Zimmerman posed these questions in their chapter on 'Gifted Women' in Joan Freeman's book **'The Psychology of Gifted Children'**, *(John Wiley & Sons, 1985):*

> *a) Are approximately equal numbers of boys and girls being identified? If not, why not? Are the selection procedures biased or the provision more attractive to one sex than the other?*
>
> *b) Do girls and boys who participate in educational provision for the gifted achieve equally well? If not, why not?*
>
> *c) Are efforts made to use non-sexist instructional materials and language laid down in the programme? If not, why not?*
>
> *d) Are girls and boys encouraged to participate in intellectual risk-taking activities to the same degree? If not, why not?*
>
> *e) Are the expectations, aspirations and confidence levels of boys and girls in the class about the same? If not, why not?*

- Fund the participation in enrichment activities by able children from materially poor backgrounds.
- Make study facilities available for able children with no privacy to work at home.
- Liaise with the medical profession to identify, and then take remedial action for, able pupils with physical handicaps.
- Provide a good pastoral care system for all pupils including the most able, both those succeeding and those underachieving.

Pastoral care

KEY MESSAGE
Many able and talented children are very contented and happy and they are well integrated into the school community.

It is important to make this point. However there are also a number of areas of conflict and concern. For able children, like all children, the teacher remains the key figure, especially in the primary sector where contact is with one main person. This theme is developed considerably in Section Five of this book: Personnel.

The pupil-teacher relationship
This relationship is central to the well-being of the child. The able child can appear a threat to the teacher who lacks confidence. It is somewhat disconcerting to have in your class someone half your size who is intellectually more capable than yourself.
A particular attitude of mind is needed to accommodate the situation without producing tension, which in turn can lead to discipline problems or difficult relationships. As teachers we need to accept that a number of children will pass through our hands who are more able than we are in a number of ways.

> *A world in which I was really (and not merely by a useful legal fiction) 'as good as everyone else', in which I never looked up to anyone wiser or cleverer or braver or more learned than I, would be insufferable.*

C.S. Lewis

Many able children go through school without too many concerns. But there are others who have found school quite an ordeal. The opening paragraph of Robert Morley's biography '**Larger Than Life**' by Margaret Morley *(Robson Books, 1979)*, illustrates how some children do not fit in with other children or with what is expected of them in terms of behaviour.

> *Some people do not make very good children. They should spring upon the world fully grown, preferably with a gin and tonic in hand, a conversation in full swing, and a camera equipped with sound on the premises to record the event. Childhood is for them a waiting game they never asked to play and one whose rules they neither accept nor indeed ever quite understand. Most people come to terms with this and give in – others won't or can't, so the period from birth to majority becomes one of agony. To none of their peers can they relate. Children's conversation is meaningless and school merely entrenches the horror.*

For some children there needs to be an extra dimension in pastoral care. It is not a case of 'going easy' or 'being soft' but of having an empathy which allows a productive pupil-teacher relationship to flourish. Consider this extract from Nicholas Evans' novel, '**The Horse Whisperer**':

> *'Dancing and riding, it's the same damn thing,' he would say. 'It's about trust and consent. You've gotten hold of one another. The man's leading but he's not dragging her, he's offering a feel and she feels it and goes with him. You're in harmony and moving to each other's rhythm, just following the feel.'*

© *Nicholas Evans 1994. Extracted from '***The Horse Whisperer***', published by Corgi, a division of Transworld Publishers Ltd. All rights reserved.*

This conveys much of what is needed in working with able children. It is about mutual respect and dignity. The teacher has a key role in accommodating such individuals within the organisation of a large institution which can become inflexible and unwelcoming unless we take care.

KEY MESSAGE
Some able children can get lost in the system and become 'loners'. They do not always fit in easily. It is worth going the extra mile to make them feel comfortable so that they can do their best.

The basis for decision-making

The teacher often has to make critical decisions about the able child. Should he or she miss out a year, take an examination early, take on extra subjects, work with older pupils or miss out steps in a programme? It is vital that the whole person is taken into consideration.

KEY MESSAGE

When important decisions are taken all aspects of the child should be taken into consideration, not just the intellect. The social and emotional well-being of the child is equally important.

As an example, a Physical Education Department in a secondary school or an individual responsible for that area of the curriculum in a primary school has important pastoral care issues when designing a policy document - e.g.:

- **How much motivation is coming from the child and how much from a parent?**
- **When a pupil has great potential in a particular sport without knowing how far they could go, how much of a lead should the PE teacher take?**
- **For a child with tremendous ability in one activity, how far should the specialism be allowed and how far should breadth be maintained?**
- **With a pupil of precocious ability, how much physical activity should be permitted, given that 'burn-out' is a real possibility?**

These are difficult questions with no easy answers but they are certainly part of the pastoral responsibility of the teacher.

A partnership with parents

Pastoral care is a joint concern. An understanding partnership between the school and the parents can best produce encouragement and support for the child.

> *Ideally, those people professionally concerned with children, and the parents of those children, should co-operate and pool the knowledge gained from their different situations so as to benefit the object of their concern, a particular child.*

Frieda Painter, **'Parent News – For the Parents of Bright Children'** no.4, May 1986

But there is a potential conflict:

Parents feel that the school does not listen and will not be flexible enough to satisfy individual needs and therefore their children *"suffer particular deprivation"* (in the words of the National Association for Gifted Children).

Schools feel that parents have an unrealistic view of how much attention can be given to the needs of a particular individual, seeing 'ability', especially if 'legitimised' by an IQ score, as a stick to beat them.

However, there are things that can be done to help prevent or resolve this conflict:

Parents can try to:
1. Recognise the difficulties of the school in terms of multiple demands within a limited budget.
2. Refrain from browbeating the school by name-dropping and quoting raw statistics.
3. Supply information to help inform the teachers about the child's particular talents.
4. Ensure that a particular course of action is followed for the child's benefit, not for the reputation nor satisfaction of the parents.

Schools can:

1. Give parents the opportunity to make nominations as part of the identification process (see Section Three).
2. Take note of the point already reached by the individual child rather than work to the normal chronological point.
3. Keep parents informed of developments in the Individual Education Plan (see Section Six).
4. Recognise that able pupils will produce joy and excitement but they may also be the cause of much stress and concern in some families, which can result in strained relations with school unless the problems are tackled.

KEY MESSAGE

As in many other situations, lack of communication between the parents of able children and schools can produce conflict, which is in nobody's best interest, least of all the child's. Simple courtesies and a genuine attempt to understand the other person's viewpoint can result in a cooperative partnership which smooths the path to effective provision.

In conclusion

☛ A major problem in many schools is the level of underachievement of some able children.

☛ Schools need to identify the cause of the underachievement – personal, family, peer pressure – and take remedial steps.

☛ A formal system involving an Underachieving Pupil Referral Sheet can help to bring collective pressure to bear upon the problem.

☛ A positive school ethos in which achievement is accepted, is not easy to establish but it is important.

☛ Pastoral care of able children is just as important as care for their intellectual needs.

☛ As with all children, a partnership between parents and the school can do much to relieve any anxieties that able pupils have.

Section Five

Personnel: the people who make a difference

This section will explore:

➡ the huge importance for able and talented children of understanding and challenging classroom teachers

➡ the problems resulting from the gaps that still remain in Initial Teacher Training and how those gaps can be overcome

➡ the crucial role of the teacher despite the many pressures, especially that of time

➡ how incremental steps allow sustainable progress

➡ the necessity for a Co-ordinator for Able and Talented Pupils, with a carefully constructed job description and with at least a modest budget line

➡ how the classroom teacher can be supported by other people

Effective provision stands or falls on the number of classroom teachers who carry out policies and procedures to the benefit of their able pupils. By themselves, written documents and systems achieve nothing. It is, therefore, of supreme importance that the classroom teacher is well trained, properly resourced and strongly supported.

A number of authors over a number of years have recognised this key role of the teacher, as the following quotes illustrate:

> *The personality, skill and experience of the teacher is a key factor in the learning situation of any pupil, but critical in the case of the gifted child. Ability to provide stimulating dialogue depends upon the degree of insight into the subject in hand.*

'Gifted and Outstanding Children' *(City of Birmingham LEA, 1978)*

> *All the work done at LEA and school level is an attempt to respond to the needs of and give support to the class teacher, for it is his or her expertise which will in the final analysis allow children to fulfil their potential.*

'Enriching and Extending The National Curriculum', *D Eyre & T Marjoram (Kogan Page, 1990)*

> *The essence of teaching is in communication, and I am presenting a plea here for a genuine meeting of minds – the exciting minds of teacher and pupil. Education for the gifted is not just a matter of dispensing ever more refined pearls of wisdom, nor of fitting pupils for high-flying careers. As with all children, it has a profound and echoing psychological impact on their feelings about themselves. Like other children, the highly able need teaching of a sufficient quality to promote their development – intellectually, emotionally, and spiritually. Successful teaching for learning helps children to a sense of control over both the learning situation and themselves, and there is ample evidence to show that this involves guidance by the teacher. And the gifted children want it too.*

'Gifted Children Growing Up', *Joan Freeman (Cassell, 1991)*

Two main problems for the classroom teacher

1 Overload

The classroom teacher has been bombarded from all sides. There have been many changes and initiatives. These have caused overload and a huge pressure in terms of time.

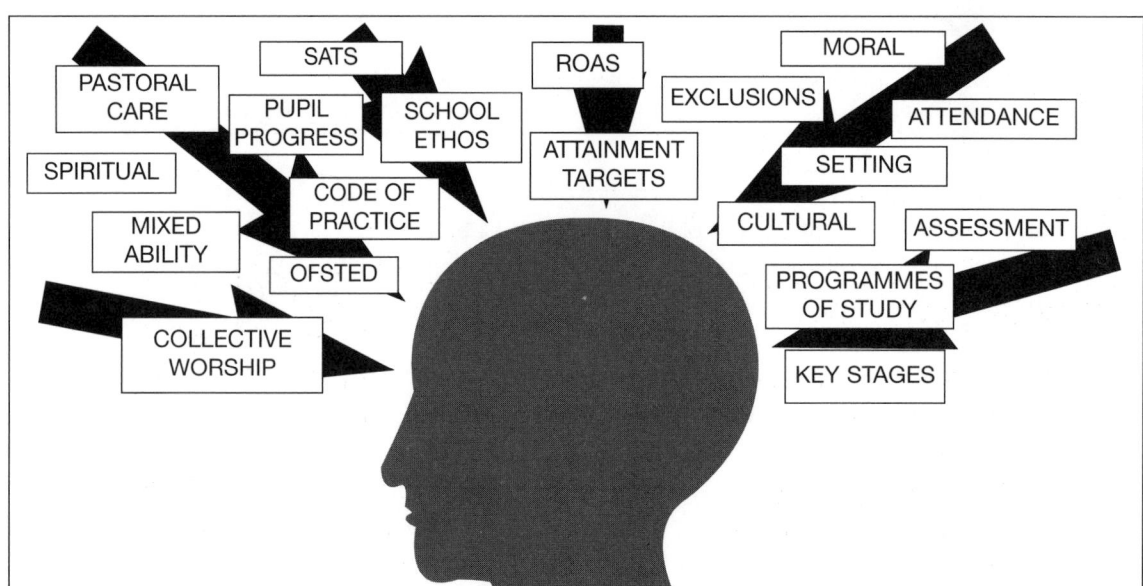

KEY MESSAGE
If the classroom teacher is to play the central role in effective provision, help is needed in terms of time and support.

2 Lack of training

Initial Teacher Training has not yet addressed the issue of preparing classroom practitioners for work with able and talented pupils. To illustrate this point, try this experiment:

When you are together with a largish group of colleagues, on an Inservice occasion or at a conference, ask how many received help on able pupils in their initial training and if so, how much was involved.

The likely result (from the author's experience of doing this experiment on many occasions) is that 5 - 10% will claim to have had some training in this area, but the huge majority of these will say that the total time allotted did not amount to more than a day or so.

In 1991 Dr George Ilsley conducted a survey of provision in initial teaching institutions on behalf of the National Association for Able Children in Education (NACE). The report concluded:

> *Almost all responding institutions purport to include the 'able' in their initial training courses, but the majority for various reasons presently give very little space in their courses to the needs of the children who are the focus of this survey, at best including them as a minor implication in teaching other parts of the course, on the assumption that their educational needs are delivered to the student teachers in a meaningful context.*

> *There is evidence internal and external to this questionnaire to indicate that the needs of the able are traditionally of low priority in comparison to those of physical handicap and other forms of special needs.*

'Educating Able Children in England and Wales – Training the Teacher,
(NACE, 1991)

Since then there has been progress but much remains to be done. Perhaps the higher profile now attached to provision for able and talented children (as discussed in the Introduction of this book) will help.

Ten ways to help the classroom teacher

1. For future generations in the profession, look to making proper provision of a reasonable content and length within Initial Teacher Training.

2. For those already qualified, increase the number and quality of Inservice courses available or direct a greater proportion of Inservice money to this area, allowing schools to buy into expertise elsewhere.

3. Provide classroom teachers with the opportunity to observe good practice elsewhere in the school or in other institutions.

4. Enable teachers to see examples of outstanding work by able children either in a material form or by means of observing at enrichment sessions.

5. Collect and disseminate case studies on both identification and provision involving both pastoral and curricular considerations.

6. Support the work in the classroom by an infra-structure involving a Co-ordinator, the Senior Management Team, governors and personnel from outside the school.

7. Establish a budget line to support enrichment in all its forms.

8. Work with national associations, the LEA or clusters of neighbouring schools to establish banks of resources and materials for teachers to inspect.

9. Assist hard-pressed teachers by purchasing enrichment materials ready for use.

10. Provide time for teachers to write their own enrichment materials which answer the individual needs of the particular school.

Incremental steps

Teachers attending courses on effective provision for the able and talented sometimes express horror at the enormity of what needs to be done. A good, full Inservice session can worry them as well as inspire them. The danger is that the teacher feels overwhelmed by the task to hand and therefore does not make any progress at all. However, it is important to make a start – however small. As we progress the task will become ever more manageable. Many schools and teachers will, in any case, not be at the start but will already be on the road.

An appropriate limerick:

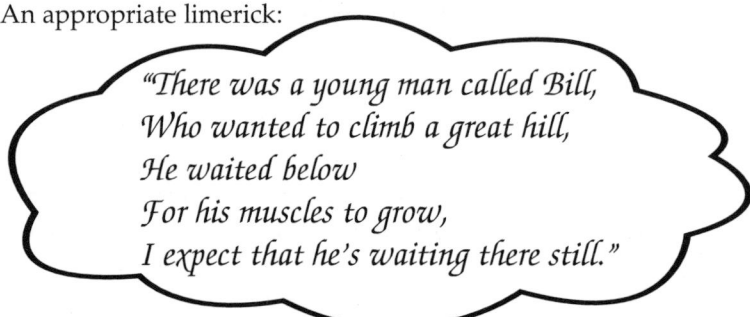

"*There was a young man called Bill,*
Who wanted to climb a great hill,
He waited below
For his muscles to grow,
I expect that he's waiting there still."

(Source unknown, but heard quoted by Mr. David Smith, one-time Plymouth Argyle manager.)

To further illustrate this message, imagine you are at point A and you wish to reach a much higher level at point B. There are different ways of getting there:

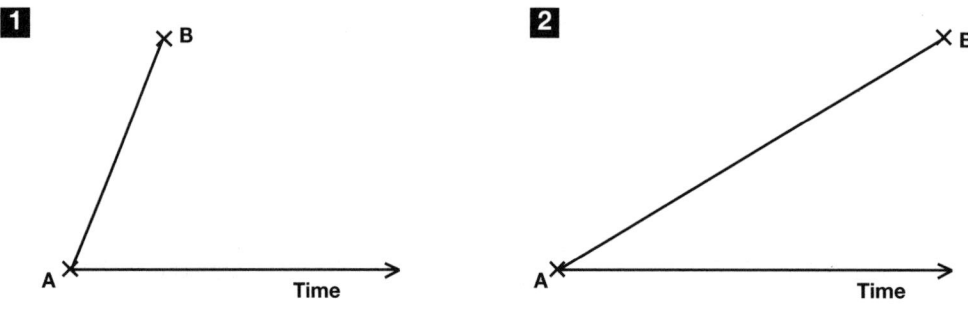

In scenario 2 it takes longer to get to point B but perhaps there is a greater chance of getting there because the programme is sustainable. Of course if you never take a step forward from A you will be there for ever.

So, where to start?

A good first step would be perhaps to try just one of the following:

- **Take one plan of action from this book, or another on the subject, and put it into operation in your school.**
- **Build up some simple resources by saving the puzzle page from the Saturday or Sunday newspaper.**
- **Look carefully at just one able child in your class and his or her needs.**
- **Take one specific area from a work scheme and examine it critically in terms of provision for the most able.**
- **Take one existing resource and find some additional challenging uses.**

You will probably find that the one idea/resource/child/section/use turns into two and three and more without your having to try too hard. This is because the task becomes easier once you have a foundation upon which to build, and when you have evidence of progress.

Now exchange your example with a like-minded colleague and you both have double. Involve a third person and you have treble.

The role of the Co-ordinator for Able and Talented Pupils

Why the need for a Co-ordinator?
Some schools already have a Co-ordinator for Able and Talented Pupils but the majority still do not. Indeed some question the importance of this role. Yet no school questions the need for somebody to co-ordinate work on Mathematics, English, Science etc., and each school will have a SENCO – a Special Educational Needs Co-ordinator. If we are serious about effective provision at both ends of the spectrum, the role of the Able and Talented Co-ordinator is just as important as that of the SENCO. The following scenarios illustrate why.

If your school has an 'average' intake going evenly across the ability range, the pupils can be represented as fitting under a normal distribution curve of intelligence.

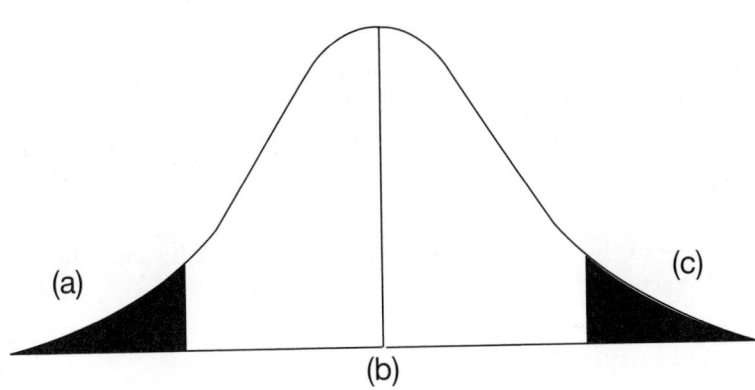

The SENCO will spend a great deal of time with the pupils in section (a) but he or she and colleagues will also deal with children to the right of (a) on the curve because:

1. A curve of intelligence only tells part of the story and children with a higher IQ will also need help.
2. Even children in section (c) can experience particular problems with which they need help.

Let us now take the reverse of this position. A Co-ordinator for Able and Talented Pupils is required to look after the needs of the pupils in section (c) but he or she and colleagues will also deal with children to the left of (c) on the curve because:

1. Pupils of limited intellectual ability may well have great talent in specific areas.
2. Most children are not able across the board but rather are very able in specific areas.

Let us also note that some children in section (a), receiving considerable attention from the SENCO, could also qualify for attention in area (c) if the curve represents say artistic ability or musical ability rather than intelligence. More will appear in section (c) on both counts but there will be pupils who are viewed in very different ways depending on the criteria used.

Different schools with different catchment areas and populations will not fit the curve drawn above. A more favoured intake will skew the curve to the right of (b), increasing the number of children in section (c). A less favoured intake will skew the curve to the left of (b), decreasing the number of children in section (c).

Whichever of these three scenarios applies, it is important that there is a Co-ordinator to look after the needs of able pupils.

- **An average intake school will have as much work to be done at the end right section as at the end left section.**
- **A school with an advantaged intake will have a large number of able pupils needing help.**
- **A school with a disadvantaged intake will have less able pupils but it will be extremely important that their needs are not overlooked.**

Could the SENCO be the Co-ordinator?

This is a possibility and many schools follow such a pattern. There are however two concerns which might suggest that a second person is needed:

1. Not all SENCOs feel comfortable in dealing with the most able because of deficiencies in training.
    Answer: Organise the necessary training? Even so some holders of the post still have reservations.

2. More critical is the question of work overload especially since the advent of the Code of Practice.

A suggested job description for the Co-ordinator

1. **Advise on revision to the school policy, especially with regard to changes in local and national conditions.**
2. **Liaise with departments on their own policies and procedures, especially subject checklists.**
3. **Make suggestions as to the Inservice needs of departments and individuals and help deliver the resulting Inservice.**
4. **Promote the use of pupil referral sheets.**
5. **Gather other information relating to identification of able and talented children.**
6. **Establish the register of able and talented pupils and make regular updates to the register.**
7. **Communicate with the parents of able and talented pupils at appropriate times.**
8. **Be available for consultation with parents at parents' evenings.**
9. **Co-ordinate the drawing up of Individual Education Plans.**
10. **Carry out reviews on pre-arranged dates.**

11. Organise enrichment activities where feasible and assist departments with the administration of their enrichment activities.
12. Promote the use of competitions, clubs and special events in tandem with the appropriate department.
13. Liaise with other phases to ensure continuity and good communication.
14. Liaise with relevant associations and other external agencies.
15. Keep a check on educational literature to bring items of interest to the attention of other staff.
16. Establish a resource bank of suitable materials.
17. Encourage the writing of enrichment materials to suit the school's needs.
18. Work with the school library and other resource bases within the school.
19. Develop community links to assist effective provision.
20. Manage an enrichment budget line.
21. Monitor and evaluate the work and suggest improvements to the Headteacher.

An enrichment budget line

Money is often tight but, even so, a number of schools have an enrichment line. It is further recognition of the need for this type of work and its importance. Such a line can be used to:

- Pay for cover staff when school staff are involved in special enrichment sessions
- Help provide INSET
- Pay membership fees for organisations such as the National Association for Able Children in Education (NACE)
- Send representation to suitable conferences
- Provide prizes for competitions
- Pay for pupils' entry fees to masterclasses and similar events
- Subscribe to journals particularly dealing with the education of the able and talented
- Support the participation of able children in special events when they come from financially poor homes
- Support a student newspaper or subject magazine
- Purchase individual copies of books and other enrichment materials to supplement departmental budgets

It could be argued that such a budget line only transfers money from one pocket to another. However this method does ensure that a part of the total school budget is spent on provision for the able and talented.

Support from other people

The Senior Management Team

A positive lead from the Headteacher and other members of the Senior Management Team is vital to give the programme status, resources and credibility. In today's changed climate it would be unsound not to give sufficient weight to the education of able and talented pupils. Close links with, and support for, the Co-ordinator are particularly important.

The governors

The governors' curricular responsibilities clearly extend to able pupils. They should be aware of particular recommendations as detailed in the Introduction to this book. Here are two other suggestions:

- It would be sensible to have a governor specifically linked to the able and talented pupils programme. This might be the same person who deals with Special Education Needs in general.
- Some areas have organised training sessions on this area of work. If that has not happened, some thought might be given to training governors.

There is an excellent NACE/DfEE booklet available called **'School Governors and More Able Children'** written by Deborah Eyre. It is of more general application than its title suggests.

A link person in each department

Where the school is large enough to accommodate such an arrangement it is helpful for each department to have one member with particular responsibility for able and talented pupils.

The LEA

Some LEAs such as Devon and Surrey have county-wide policies which support the work of individual institutions. There are often designated advisory staff who specialise in this area of work. Find out what is available in your area.

External agencies

The most supportive group for teachers is the National Association for Able Children in Education whose personnel have been making a substantial contribution from the days of the Schools Council. NACE produces a journal and a newsletter and there is a range of publications for purchase. The annual conference moves around geographically and there are also regional events. Members can ask for advice from the association's office in Oxford where materials are available for inspection.

A number of other organisations can provide useful assistance – Longlands, Aganippe, Kilve Court, National Association for Gifted Children (the parents' based group), Scott Hurd, GIFT and Mensa – and their enrichment activities are described in Section Seven of this book. (Addresses can be found on p.101-102). NB This is a sample only – there are many other agencies.

National Associations for subject areas also provide materials, ideas and support.

KEY MESSAGE
If work is of sufficient importance it must be supported by leadership, resources, INSET and a suitable infra-structure. The classroom teacher deserves this backing to make effective provision a reality.

In conclusion

- ☞ The importance of the classroom teacher to the wellbeing of the able child cannot be over-emphasised.

- ☞ Many teachers have not received help and advice on dealing with able and talented pupils in their initial training and therefore it is essential that they are assisted now.

- ☞ Within the competing pressures for time and attention this area of work should not be neglected.

- ☞ It is all too easy to be overwhelmed by all that needs to be done, but small, incremental steps do eventually make a difference.

- ☞ Co-ordination of this work is a substantial undertaking and it is best done by creating a discrete post.

- ☞ There are a number of other key people who can assist in effective provision – the Senior Management Team, governors, the LEA, and external agencies – including the relevant national associations.

Section Six

Effective provision in the classroom

In this section you will see that:

➡ the decisions relating to grouping policy, on whether to employ streaming, setting, mixed ability or extraction, are important considerations in terms of provision

➡ Individual Education Plans set targets to be achieved by activities within the classroom and beyond

➡ the teacher needs to plan the work in the classroom as part of the totality of what the able child is experiencing, and ensure that this classroom provision has both pastoral and academic considerations

➡ able pupils need to be challenged and therefore the presentation and demands of work have to be carefully thought out

➡ particular pieces of work can not only be used directly but can also serve a valuable purpose as examplars that point the way to effective provision in the classroom

Most contact with, and teaching of, able and talented pupils takes place in the normal classroom – a theme developed strongly in Section Seven: Enrichment activities. The classroom is where everything is pulled together: theory (see Section One) underlies the practice; identification strategies (see Section Three) include teacher observation; Individual Education Plans (discussed in this section) are kept in the classroom and put to use there; the school ethos (see Section Four) is reflected in the atmosphere of the classroom; appropriate resources (see Section Nine) are employed there to produce excellent responses; the main monitoring and evaluating procedures (see Section Eight) also take place in the classroom.

Grouping policy
The way children are grouped for work is an important decision. The various options need careful consideration.

Streaming
This is a 'non-starter'. Research by many people over a period of time shows that only a few children are able 'across the board' and that most have a talent in a particular area or areas. Streaming is therefore the method which guarantees the greatest number of people being placed in the wrong group.

Setting
Setting is used extensively to pull together pupils of like ability. This method of organisation tends to make teachers feel more secure but there are some difficulties associated with it:

1. Some pupils finish up wrongly in the top set because inappropriate identification takes place.

2. Once the sets have been formed they tend to remain too rigidly in place.

3. Schools take the view that once setting has taken place the job is done.

4. Setting is not carried out in a consistent manner throughout the school.

Suggested solutions:

1. Departments discuss what is meant by high ability in their subject and then ensure that the 'essential ingredients of ability' are reflected in the tests, or other methods used, for selection. Subject checklists can make a valuable contribution here. The most obvious example is not to use only arithmetic tests to set Mathematics groups.

2. Even though some difficult discussions with parents and pupils will result, there should be freedom to move children between sets if further evidence suggests that such a move is desirable.

3. Setting is regarded as only one part of the solution. The sets thus formed should not be treated as a homogeneous group but rather as a group of individuals whose abilities will differ, even in the one set.

4. The Able and Talented Co-ordinator monitors pupil setting against prior achievement data and queries any mismatch of ability and set. Senior Management Teams must have a clear policy on whose decision prevails – other departments' or the Co-ordinator's – and the criteria for that decision.

Mixed ability

Mixed ability grouping avoids the problems of selection – or does it? Actually it doesn't because the school has to select pupils to form a balance in each group. Teachers find mixed ability groups difficult to deal with in terms of provision but, even so, many of them find the concept philosophically acceptable. One great advantage is that children cannot be missed through selection procedures and then excluded from the curricular provision that follows.

The main criticism traditionally centres upon the failure to satisfy all abilities within the group, with an accusation that the system tends to be directed at the average ability members of the group. Able pupils are not stretched sufficiently and those with learning problems struggle to cope. This, in a sense, goes back to the supposed advantage given at the end of the paragraph above, because children can be excluded from suitable curricular provision – due to lack of recognition and planning *inside* the group rather than by being omitted from the group of able pupils.

The solution? Demanding as it might be professionally, teachers have to prepare material and plan lessons to make effective provision for all group members including the most able.

KEY MESSAGE

When streaming is ruled out (correctly), a common theme emerges. Both setting and mixed ability teaching require individual provision for able and talented pupils, within the group.

Extraction

Another possibility is to extract able pupils from the normal classroom situation in order to form a special group. This can be seen as similar to extraction of those with marked learning problems. One particularly good feature of this system is that it brings very able pupils together, which many educationalists would say is necessary to satisfy one of the needs of such children. It does however tend to be more divisive than methods which handle the situation within the normal class. Peer pressure could be increased, although perhaps the real answer is a school ethos in which such a practice becomes accepted as reasonable and appropriate.

The individual child in the classroom

Here is a suggested format for an Individual Education Plan for Able and Talented Pupils.

<u>Individual Education Plan – Able and Talented Pupils</u>

Name:

Date of Birth:

Area(s) of the Curriculum/Activities Involved

Background Evidence (summary only)

Action to be Taken/Targets

Review Date

The key section of the document is that concerned with *action*. This is the means to delivering effective provision on an individual pupil basis. As a result the sheet has a section for targets, with review dates, so that individual able pupil progress is planned and monitored. As with all suggested documents for a Shadow Code of Practice we are looking to effective provision through a modest level of paperwork, using forms that are easy to use and which do not deter the teacher from filling them in.

General and subject checklists are not just helpful for identification – they can also be used to inform the IEPs. For example, a checklist which notes ability to deal with the abstract as a characteristic of able pupils, leads to provision that involves algebra, proverbs, codes, allegories and the like.

The teacher has to plan a programme inside school that is linked to and complements provision beyond the classroom so that there is a meaningful totality. Let us take Art as an example and examine how such a programme could be devised.

<u>Component A:</u> *A subject checklist*

The first step is to consider a checklist of characteristics associated with artistically gifted children in order to help identify the target group. **'Gifted Children in Middle and Comprehensive Secondary Schools'**, *(HMSO, 1977)*, suggested some common characteristics:

> *● Have an interest often amounting to an obsession with visual recording, matching the world around them to images which they create.*
> *● Have an ability to depict in a way which is illuminating or revealing, seeing or emphasising unexpected relationships between colours or shapes.*
> *● Either have, or readily acquire the draughtsmanship, manual and physical skills or techniques they need to convey their message. They are sensitive to the quality of materials and tools they use. This is different from the facile competence some pupils have which is more concerned with the means than the message.*

Bruce Hurn, former HMI, writing as NAGC Art Consultant in the Autumn 1995 journal of that association, looked at special abilities for art and design becoming apparent through many and various forms, such as:

● a quite remarkable ability for expressive and personal use of colour
● an extraordinary ability to observe and record in line and tone
● demonstration of a quite exceptional visual imagination through drawings, paintings, modelling or constructional activities

<u>Component B:</u> *Provision in the classroom*

Bruce Hurn argues that because different pupils demonstrate their great talent in a number of ways:

> *The importance of well balanced, carefully structured schemes of work and a rich variety of art and design experiences throughout all four key stages can hardly be overemphasised.*

The HMI book **'Gifted Children in Middle and Comprehensive Secondary Schools'** *advises that very able artists "need the opportunity – and sufficient time – to choose and to practice in their own field."* Other needs are also suggested:

● their practice and achievements should be challenged and appraised with vigour and frankness by teachers
● access to books and periodicals in variety for study in breadth
● the chance to work side by side with other gifted pupils
● a school ethos which tolerates idiosyncrasies and promotes originality through the freedom to be original

<u>Component C</u>: *What else should happen in and out of school?*
'Setting the Scene: The Arts and Young People' *(Department of National Heritage, 1996)* states that:

> *Children and young people should have opportunities to:*
>
> - *observe, work with and be taught by professional artists, craftspeople, designers and architects*
> - *visit local and national galleries, museums, studios and exhibitions on a regular basis*
> - *join art clubs in school or locally*
> - *have their work displayed in exhibitions*
> - *enter local, regional and national art competitions*

(**'Setting the Scene: The Arts and Young People'** also deals with Music, Dance, Drama and Literature, looking at both National Curriculum entitlement and *"what else should happen in and out of school"*.)

The pastoral and academic role overlap
Section Four discussed the importance of the pupil-teacher relationship and stressed that critical decisions about the child are about much more than the care of the intellect or specific ability. Any section on the classroom needs to remind us of this key point. Let us add some further considerations to the earlier material.

1 <u>Expectations</u>
A number of pieces of research have stressed the importance of the teacher's expectations and how these tend to be self-fulfilling. **'Could Do Better'**, edited by Patrick Dickinson *(Arrow Books/Save the Children, 1982)*, has a wonderful example about Bob Paisley, once the manager of the Liverpool football team.

> *I have vivid memories of the woodwork lesson and the Master who went with it. The weekly lesson always began in the same way. Each pupil produced his individual work while the Master pronounced judgement on the exercise. The best model was always highly praised and it was always made by the same boy. When my turn came to make the long walk to the back of the room with my effort the humiliation always ended with the word 'disgraceful'.*
>
> *It was arranged one week that I should take up the model made by the expert woodworker. As I stood confidently expecting at least nine out of ten, the rest of the class fell about when the dreaded words were uttered:*
> *'Paisley, this is disgraceful!'*

Try this experiment – mark a set of work deliberately avoiding the name of the child.

Look to open windows not close doors.

2 <u>Some characteristics will result in tensions</u>
Encouraging able children to express themselves has consequences which we must be prepared to accommodate. For example, in Section Three there was a suggested subject checklist for History. Able historians are sceptical about evidence. They do not necessarily believe what they are told. They are expected to doubt and to challenge.

Effective Provision for Able & Talented Children

These qualities, valued in History lessons, may also lead the child into situations of dispute where the teacher, or other adult, might suspect 'cheek' or disobedience.

3 Inspiration and perspiration

Success comes not just from raw talent but also from application and hard work. Stephen Spender says about writing poetry:

> *Inspiration is the beginning of a poem and it is also its final goal. It is the final idea which drops into the poet's mind and it is the final idea which he at last achieves in words. In between this start and this winning post there is the hard race, the sweat and toil.*

'**The Creative Process: A Symposium**', *B Ghiselin (ed.))University of California Press, 1952)*

KEY MESSAGE
To help the able child's creativity the teacher needs to provide not only the right opportunities and stimuli but also the support to see it through.

The needs of able pupils

Academic and pastoral demands overlap and intertwine, and the teacher in the classroom has the responsibility of trying to satisfy them all. Many of the academic needs of able pupils are detailed later but let us also note that the pupil needs:

- **to be treated as a child of a particular chronological age no matter what his or her intellectual level may be**
- **to receive reward and praise in the same way as all other children**
- **to sometimes 'slip' in terms of behaviour without their ability being held against them**

The National Association for Gifted Children suggests in its booklet '**Foundation for NAGC Leaders**' three consequences of needs not being recognised and provided for:

> - *some will react against the boredom and frustration with poor behaviour, anger etc.*
> - *others will become introverted and, in time, depressed*
> - *peer pressure to conform or low teacher expectation, or both, may lead some to the effective 'switching off' of mental activity with quiet resignation*

Teaching strategies

Here are some suggestions:

> **1.** Instead of a common approach to all, judge the correct starting-point for each child, taking into account the progress already made by the child, including work done at home. An obvious example is to take account of early reading development achieved by the infant before starting school.
>
> **2.** Allow children to miss out stages when it is clear that they have the ability to jump steps needed by the great majority. The alternative is to appear punitive – i.e. 'you must do this whether or not it will do you any good because everybody follows that route'.

3. Give space for individual pupils to experiment so that an original way of working is not discouraged. This fits the spirit of this quote from Thoreau:

   "If a man does not keep pace with his companions, perhaps it is because he hears a different drummer. Let him step to the music he hears, however measured or far away."

4. Create as many open-ended situations as possible. This allows able children to show themselves by individual responses which may be very different from others produced in their class.

5. Be prepared to cut short the amount of practice of a particular skill or process if an able child shows an early mastery. Use the time so produced to allow for other development, either in depth or in breadth.

6. Allow the able child to work independently, but not become 'out of touch'. Often the child will see a way of taking the work on to new stages. This is to be encouraged. However, able children do still need contact with their teachers even if the time spent is differently targetted.

7. Take advantage of the detailed and advanced knowledge which a child might have by allowing him or her to be a partner in the delivery of the lesson. This is a good way of dealing with the worries felt by some teachers that an able child knows more than they themselves do.

8. Design some tasks so that there are more advanced tasks available only for those who complete the earlier sections easily and well.

9. Have available exciting and challenging materials for relatively short periods of time so that an able child finishing early has something worthwhile to do next.

10. Use differentiated homeworks to give able children a more demanding target, or sometimes encourage attempts at work that the rest of the class is not going to do.

11. Employ different levels of language, especially when in one-to-one conversations. Use more elaborate language and an extended vocabulary for those for whom it is appropriate, including within written instructions.

12. The more able the child, the less instruction you provide. This is part of a larger process of setting work for able children which is deliberately more difficult and more challenging (see below).

Underpinning the curriculum

The atmosphere within the classroom

If the school takes a joint approach to provision for able pupils the role of the individual teacher is helped. Even so he or she can do much him or her self to create an encouraging and challenging atmosphere within the classroom.

Enjoyment is a key ingredient. Martin Gardner, one of the world's greatest exponents of entertaining material for Mathematics and Science, quotes in the introduction to his book **'Further Mathematical Diversions'**, *(Penguin, 1969)*, a 'grook' from Piet Hein's **'Grooks'**, *(Cambridge, Mass: MIT Press, 1966):*

> *"Taking fun as simply fun and earnestness in earnest shows how thoroughly thou none of the two discernest."*

There could be no better way of expressing the sentiment that enjoyment in education can serve very serious purposes.

Celebration of the subject can be achieved partly through good display. The environment needs to present excitement and challenge. A weekly puzzle or competition on the wall, exhibitions of unusual visual material, the stimulus of the provocative quotation – these and many more items set the tone and create an expectation in the pupils.

Another feature of great significance is the encouragement to experiment intellectually, to take risks and to cope with failure.

> *"To dare is to lose your foothold for a moment: not to dare is to lose yourself."*

Soren Kierkegaard

Involvement of the pupils themselves

Try the following approaches to involve pupils more fully in their own education and to benefit from their perceptions:

- encourage peer nomination (see Section Three)
- involve the able pupil in teaching the class
- allow scope in exercises for development of the work by the pupils
- organise group work to discuss various solutions and ways forward when a problem has been set, and then to report back
- ask able pupils to devise the next stages of the work
- after playing a game, ask pupils to design their own
- encourage pupils to suggest improvement to products, procedures and organisation
- ensure that pupils play a part in mapping out the route forward in their own learning programme

Making the most of the National Curriculum

There have been problems as well as opportunities resulting from the introduction and subsequent development of the National Curriculum. Let us look at the positive aspects:

1. The basic philosophy that differentiation would be promoted so that work matches more closely pupils' abilities.

2. The enabling statement in each subject order highlights the need for able pupils to use material from a later key stage than the one they are in chronologically.

3.	The inclusion of an Exceptional Performance paragraph beyond level Eight is an encouragement to consider what high ability produces in a specific subject area. The paragraphs tend to be rather mechanistic, probably because of their construction from a level-to-level development. A more natural approach is to create a synthesis of the subject checklist. The department's own paragraph set alongside the one in the National Curriculum allows ownership, promotes a better understanding and acts as a useful piece of Inservice work.

4.	Many of the phrases and sentences do fit easily into a curriculum which is suitable to challenge the most able. Some of the ideas are transferrable into other curriculum areas (see Section One).

Key curriculum principles

1.	Tasks should not be too tightly prescribed – the able pupil needs space to develop the work.

2.	For at least a reasonable proportion of the week there needs to be real pace. The able pupil should be working with urgency, completing the large volume of work (in quality terms rather than just quantity) of which he or she is capable. Thus we can see *differentiation by pace*.

3.	A great variety of sources gives opportunity for assignments to be taken along different routes. Chris Dickinson in 'Effective Learning Activities', (*Network Educational Press, 1996*), discusses many ways of organising sources. Here we have *differentiation by resource*.

4.	Able pupils should be taken to the limits of their ability by very demanding work. Their education should not be too safe or protected.

5.	The same starting-point for various pupils is fine in many cases providing that a good proportion of the tasks set are open-ended and allow individuality of response. *Differentiation by outcome* has much merit but it is not the answer to everything.

6.	Overdirection in teaching is to be avoided but the teacher retains the key role of managing the classroom for the benefit of all pupils. The teacher's input may well be of a changed nature to allow *differentiation by support* – a method based upon the notion that some pupils need more help than others to complete the work set. Chris Dickinson in his book, talks of *differentiation by dialogue* – using different levels of vocabulary and complexity of language for different children.

7.	There needs to be heavy reliance upon the higher order thinking skills such as prediction and hypothesis. A taxonomy such as Bloom's is useful to develop a battery of appropriate words to promote – speculate, infer, imagine, judge, contrast, dissect, distinguish, predict, hypothesize, categorise, create etc.

8.	*Differentiation by input* allows either instructions in which only the able pupils reach the later tasks, or the establishment of complete exercises which are designed to be difficult and are only placed in front of the most able. The idea that unless everybody can 'have a go' then nobody should, is a nonsense.

9.	The Curriculum encompasses everything. Yes, there are legal requirements to be met in the National Curriculum. It would be helpful to have a very open mind about what does constitute suitable material. If it challenges, enriches, extends and provides enjoyment and if it satisfies the higher order thinking skills, then it is appropriate.

KEY MESSAGE
Once good curriculum principles have been established much else will automatically follow – style of work, the nature of the pupil-teacher relationship and the resources which can be used.

What makes a task or piece of work difficult and challenging?

We have talked a great deal about challenging able and talented pupils within effective provision. It seems sensible then to examine the notion of 'difficult and challenging'. When the contributing factors have been identified, then they can be used in lesson planning and creation of materials.

Here are some thoughts:

1. 'Putting it all together.' Very often children work on a single operation with considerable practice of that particular skill. More difficulty is involved if, for example, Mathematics problems link a series of different processes rather than focusing on a single process, or a passage in a foreign language has a number of components rather than sentences testing the same item.

2. Pace is a key consideration. Even relatively simple tasks are much more difficult to complete if very limited time is allowed. Another aspect of pace is the increased speed of delivery in a modern foreign language.

3. In Mathematics and Science 3-dimensional thinking is much more difficult than 2-dimensional. For example, examining and rotating a diamond structure in 3-D is more difficult than examining more simple structures in 2-D.

4. The degree of structure in a task varies the level of difficulty. Guidance through a piece of work makes it easier. Less instruction and the necessity for pupils to work out much more for themselves, increases the challenge.

5. The level of vocabulary used makes a significant difference, whether in English, other subjects written in English, or in a foreign language. Some pupils display their ability by their capacity to intuit.

6. Having to employ more than one sense at the same time is difficult. Watching a video carefully to gather visual data while picking up information from sound at the same time requires great concentration.

7. Material which has an abstract quality is a source of real challenge whether it be algebraic (which is what makes Advanced level Mathematics particularly testing), an idiom which is associated with a specific foreign language, or proverbs and allegories in English.

8. Confusing the order in which the reader can use information increases difficulty, as does the technique of making the pupil hold information for later use. There is a clear use for this technique in puzzles, problem-solving and various areas of Humanities subjects.

9. How straightforwardly a question or task is set is of great relevance. Material and work based on it can be fairly obvious or the route can be obscured by shifting or restating the problem. This applies in Science and many other subjects.

10. Previous experience helps the pupil – so tasks that are not directly related to what has gone before are harder to understand.

11. There are actions which are technically more difficult to carry out. Very high notes are harder for the singer or musical performer. Some movements in gymnastics require greater skill and dexterity than others. Quick finger movements with musical instruments also require great skill, as does controlling a ball hit on the volley.

12. The 'density' of information affects the ease, or not, of comprehension. The equivalent of this in practical activities is the density of operations such as linked manoeuvres in ice skating or gymnastics. Having to juggle many different concepts in an Advanced level Science assignment and trying to 'see the wood from the trees' in large amounts of evidence in a History or Geography investigation are other linked examples.

13. The 'disguising' of ideas and concepts makes the appreciation of a text in literature more demanding. The subtlety of the presentation, the items that are left out rather than included (so that the criticism of a character can be by omission, for example) and the use of symbols and metaphor – all of these increase the difficulty of the text.

14. If you are on less familiar territory the challenge becomes the greater. Within the many thinking skills that can be used pupils tend to operate better in some areas than others. Work is therefore more difficult when you are forced to use methods which you have not mastered, or with which you do not have a natural empathy.

KEY MESSAGE

Analyse what makes work difficult and challenging, both generally and in the specific subject. Then use the list you have produced to provide a 'menu' of techniques to be incorporated into work for able and talented pupils.

In conclusion

- ☞ Streaming cannot be justified but setting, mixed ability and extraction all have their benefits providing that their weaknesses are also known and countered.

- ☞ Individual Education Plans for able pupils allow individual monitoring and target-setting to take place, thus making a vital contribution to effective provision.

- ☞ By following good teaching strategies and taking advantage of opportunities beyond the classroom, the teacher can successfully meet the needs of able pupils.

- ☞ Able children need a positive and challenging atmosphere, a variety of differentiation techniques as well as careful pastoral care, for we are concerned about the welfare of the whole person.

- ☞ Teachers need to be aware as to what makes particular pieces of work difficult and challenging so that those principles can be employed extensively.

Particular pieces of work for use in the classroom

Here are three examples of material written specifically for able children. 'Jigsaws' involves analysis, deduction, investigation, creativity and evaluation; 'A capital idea' is a reasonably difficult code, which is good for able children because of its abstract quality; 'What if...?' could be tackled by many children but, as always, with open-ended materials, it gives scope for creativity and individuality. As commented elsewhere in the book, it is difficult and possibly unwise to set an age for the target group. Able children defy such 'boxes'.

The three particular pieces are a very small sample of the many types of exercises that can be set. In writing such materials one needs to be aware of the specific needs of able pupils, pay attention to the checklist of characteristics (see p.29-30) and answer the requirements of the National Curriculum.

'Jigsaws'

This exercise, which involves studying jigsaws of varying difficulty, is very much linked with the discussion in Section Six on what makes a piece of work difficult or challenging.

RESEARCH
Investigate the variety of jigsaws currently on sale, taking into consideration their size, shape, subject and complexity.

ACTIVITIES
1. Considering the 'normal' jigsaw puzzle (i.e. a rectangular or circular picture or photograph) write down the factors which make a particular puzzle more or less difficult to solve.

2. Some jigsaws do not have a picture of the finished puzzle to help the solution. Some of these are linked to mysteries or murders and there is an accompanying booklet of information containing clues. If you are the artist creating such a mystery puzzle, what factors must you take into account?

3. There are some puzzles which have four rectangles inserted one inside the other. How many straight sides does the solver have to take into account?

4. What techniques, other than those used in tasks 2 and 3, have you discovered manufacturers using to make their jigsaws difficult to solve?

DESIGN
You have been asked to design a jigsaw puzzle picture for a mystery. The scenario is that an identification parade is taking place and in the line-up is a suspect for a break-in at a jeweller's shop.

Either:
  a) plan the design of the picture with clear indications of what it would look like

  or, if you are a more confident artist,

  b) draw or paint the picture.

Also,

c) Write the information booklet which contains the clues that link with the picture.

FURTHER WORK

Get hold of one or more examples of 'no-picture' mystery jigsaw puzzles and attempt to find the solution. Evaluate how well the company carried out the design and execution of the product in order to accomplish its purpose.

TEACHERS' NOTES

Some suggested answers:

1. ● Many people believe that an illustration makes an easier puzzle than a photograph because of the changing shades and textures.
   ● Large patches of the same colour can make placing pieces more difficult.
   ● Items or people repeated cause problems.

2. ● The picture needs to have some obvious sections as otherwise the solver has nothing to work from. A murder mystery at Christmas for example allows the inclusion of a tree, decorations, presents etc.
   ● It is helpful to have bold patterns and clear areas of contrasting colours.
   ● There has to be great clarity especially in the section of the puzzle which gives vital clues.

3. There are 28 straight sides. For the three inner rectangles there is an inside and an outside on four sides i.e., 3x2x4=24. For the outside rectangle there are four 'inner' sides but no pieces beyond that.

4. Manufacturers have used ingenious methods including:
   ● Double-sided pieces of the same picture
   ● Pictures of multiple similar items, e.g. baked beans
   ● No straight edges at the fringes of the puzzle
   ● The picture can actually shift and does not have a set solution

OTHER POINTS

This piece of work illustrates the concept of how tasks can be made more difficult. From the solid wooden board with four shapes to fit in, right through to the devious designs described above there is a huge spectrum of difficulty.

A number of key skills are employed in 'Jigsaws' – analysis, deduction, investigation, creativity, evaluation. Hopefully, also, this is an enjoyable exercise with an interesting vehicle.

A capital idea

This exercise combines a standard topic in English – capital letters – with decoding work. This allows routine work to be dealt with in an interesting and enjoyable way.

There are two teaching strategies to be taken into consideration. Firstly the teacher needs to decide what other information should be made available alongside the exercise. If the pupils have just finished work on capital letters this exercise could be used as revision. Otherwise it may be necessary to give details on the rules for the use of capitals. Secondly the teacher needs to prompt the pupils during the decoding. Too much help spoils the trial-and-error which is an essential part of such work. On the other hand there is no merit in a child sitting for a long time and making no progress.

ACTIVITY

Early one Saturday morning Susan Holt sighed deeply as she opened her homework books. When her mother asked what was the matter Susan explained that she had to do an exercise on capital letters for school, and that she wanted instead to send out a message to her friends in the Smashing Six Secret Society. Mrs. Holt was sympathetic and suggested that Susan could make the morning more enjoyable by sending out a message in a code which was based upon the correct use of capital letters. "That way you will all get some useful practice and at the same time enjoy yourself," she said.

Susan thought that this was a great idea and below is the passage that she sent to the members of the Smashing Six Secret Society. See if you can work out what message was hidden in it. It will help if you first of all try to remember the rules for the use of capital letters. Look carefully at their position in the passage, and at whether they have been used correctly or are missing.

The passage:

immediately the Prime Minister called a cabinet meeting to discuss the threat. He was worried about security. many lives could be lost. The newspapers had not yet picked up the story but Michael best, the reporter, was aware that something was going on. The letter had been posted in otley. both the envelope and its contents had been sent for analysis. ideas and plans for action were being collected together by harry Preston. Further news was expected later in the week when attention would switch to Manchester. The tension was unbearable. emma Jones had been assigned to the case to work at the operations room in clamp Road. clearly the home of lady scott would need special supervision on the Tuesday morning.

The solution

The code works on a simple basis. Where a capital letter has been used correctly the letter before it is part of the message. Where a capital letter is missing it is the letter after it which is to be used. The message – MEET AT TEN TODAY NORMAL PLACE – is formed as shown opposite.

immediately the Prime Minister called a cabinet meeting to discuss the threat. He was worried about security. many lives could be lost. The newspapers had not yet picked up the story but Michael best, the reporter, was aware that something was going on. The letter had been posted in otley. both the envelope and its contents had been sent for analysis. ideas and plans for action were being collected together by harry Preston. Further news was expected later in the week when attention would switch to Manchester. The tension was unbearable. emma Jones had been assigned to the case to work at the operations room in clamp Road. clearly the home of lady scott would need special supervision on the Tuesday morning.

POINTS TO NOTE

1. Codes are very useful because they can be set at such difficulty that they make even able children struggle. Nobody should succeed easily all the time. Learning to cope with failure is important.
2. Codes have an abstract quality, which features strongly on checklists of characteristics of able pupils, and therefore they are very suitable work.
3. The vehicle for delivery is interesting.
4. The exercise combines a staid but necessary content with a real challenge.
5. Here is an example of good teaching practice where the contact is through a challenging piece of work. Able children need teachers' time but spent in a different way from the time spent with the less able.
6. Other content could be used with a similar code context.
7. Other aspects of punctuation or grammar could be involved with a changed basis for the code, for example, the letter above or below, or a complete word, or two letters together.
8. The amount of help can vary and therefore fits the concept of varying the number of steps along the way.
9. For a child who has already mastered the rules of capital letters this activity provides a different starting-point whilst their peers are busy with the basic work.

What if...?

This is an opportunity for imaginative work either verbally or in written form. The actual questions can be changed. Their subject matter could be very different. It is possible to base all the 'What ifs?' in a specific curriculum area, such as:

History -

> **What if Hitler had invaded Britain successfully?**
> **or**
> **What if Africa had been the first continent to experience an industrial revolution?**

OR

Science -

> **What if there was no such thing as gravity?**
> **or**
> **What if a mystery illness wiped out the mouse population of Great Britain?**

ACTIVITY

Much of the work you do at school is based upon factual materials and descriptive writing concerning set points. It is important that you are able to exercise your imagination. 'What if' presents you with such an opportunity. Try some or all of the following as a basis for creative writing and/or discussion.

What if...

1. we discovered the secret of eternal life?
2. the oceans all dried up?
3. the world's reserves of iron ore were exhausted?
4. parents could choose the characteristics and talents of future children?
5. there was another Ice Age?
6. E.T. really was left behind on earth?
7. courts in the USA accepted the right of the Red Indians to their old lands?
8. you really were given three wishes?
9. rabies spread to the British Isles?
10. Jesus returned to the Middle East today?
11. all dogs were savage and became our enemies?
12. colours changed without any warning?
13. plants could move?
14. it was light for twenty-four hours every day?
15. frost could occur in the British Isles at any time during the year?
16. you had not just one 'double' but there were twenty people who looked exactly like you?
17. print faded and disappeared after two years?
18. we had to rest for a minimum of two hours after eating anything?

Now have a go at making up your own 'What ifs'. Try to choose situations that would produce interesting consequences.

Enrichment activities

In this section you will find:

➡ that enrichment can take many forms and has been described in a variety of ways

➡ how general enrichment activities and able and talented activities overlap but why there is also a need for activities aimed specifically at the able

➡ that there is a strong rationale for enrichment sessions but that classroom activities still have prime importance

➡ the various forms enrichment activities might take, with a number of specific examples

➡ where help is available outside school

There are many variations in the interpretations of the term 'enrichment'. It has been described as:

- A higher quality of work than the norm for the age group
- Work covered in more depth
- A broadening of the learning experience
- Promoting a higher level of thinking
- The inclusion of additional subject areas and/or activities
- The use of supplementary materials beyond the normal range of resources

The descriptions themselves overlap. They also collectively overlap the other key processes such as acceleration and differentiation.

For a working definition, let's take a statement taken from **'Gifted Education: Identification and Provision'**, *David George (David Fulton Publishers, 1995),* which says that enrichment *"provides experiences and activities beyond the regular curriculum"*

Examining the overlap between general enrichment and able and talented activities

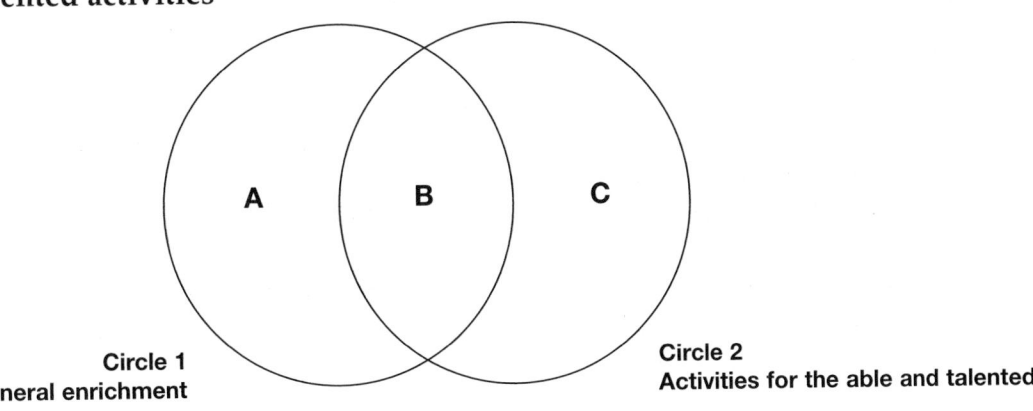

A   B   C

Circle 1
General enrichment

Circle 2
Activities for the able and talented

Area A represents activities which may go beyond the regular curriculum but they would not stretch and challenge the most able. For example, in a lower Mathematics set unusual presentations of material might be used without working at the higher levels of thinking.

Even where children are of limited ability it is always worthwhile to enrich their curriculum. For example, reading books for those experiencing major difficulties need to present relevant and interesting story lines or motivation is lost.

Area B represents activities which provide enrichment for a wide range of pupils whilst, at the same time, opening up specific opportunities for the most able. For example:

- A school musical provides enrichment for a large number of children. Productions with large casts provide a large number of parts for those with acting and singing ability, and behind the scenes many other talents can be put to work organising lighting, sound and costume design. Many so-called menial tasks are vital to the overall success of the production – scenery changes, selling refreshments, ushering members of the audience to their seats.

  For pupils with a real talent for acting and singing this would be an integral part of an Individual Education Plan, along with extended curriculum opportunities, links with community groups and possibly participation with other gifted actors/ singers/ dancers at county level.

- Book week. During such a week a host of varied activities enrich the lives of many pupils. Some of those activities provide a particular benefit to advanced readers or to aspiring writers. Competitions allow individuals to respond at their own particular level.

- Visits to the theatre, concerts, museums, field work centres etc. allow a wide spectrum of participation which contains further possibilities for those with a specific interest or talent.

- Special events such as the school sports day or swimming gala encourage entry from a largish number of children especially if there is a house, or other-based, competition resulting from the points gathered. On the day that a child of limited running, throwing or swimming ability gains at least a point for his/her team, other pupils are attempting to break records.

Area C represents enrichment activities directed at the able and talented. This allows the content to be of a much more advanced nature without concern that some children will become frustrated. Working in this way will also answer another important need – to bring together those of like mind or ability to stimulate each other. For example:

- A language day for very good modern linguists, perhaps involving a more unusual language such as Japanese.
- Sports schools of excellence where exceptional athletes or games players receive advanced coaching.
- A 'cluster' activity involving neighbouring schools and colleges bringing together their most able pupils to work in collaboration or competitively with their peers on a particular curriculum area.

The rationale behind enrichment sessions

Much enrichment takes place within the normal classroom (see Section Six). There is also a place for specially established sessions outside the normal timetable.

Ten good reasons for enrichment sessions:

1. The extended time framework allows for greater flexibility in working. The artificial control by the bell is removed.

2. There are opportunities for vertical grouping. Children of high ability from perhaps three or four years can be included.

3. More unusual elements can be included thus providing interesting vehicles.

4. There is a gathering of 'like minds'. Whatever the grouping policy of the school it is important to bring together children of high ability on at least some occasions.

5. The concept of 'celebration' is fostered. 'What can we celebrate today?' is an important message. All areas of the curriculum should be involved, not just the more obvious ones such as physical education, drama, music and dance.

6. Such sessions aid the development of an ethos of achievement, which is vital (see Section Four).

7. Enrichment sessions provide valuable Inservice possibilities for members of staff taking part or observing.

8. The organisation and outcomes of the sessions promote further discussion, which is valuable for staff understanding and development. There are many things to consider, such as:
   a) How were the participants selected?
   b) What activities went well and which were not so popular?
   c) How did the pupils feel about being selected?
   d) What reaction did they get from others?
   e) How did they feel about working with children of different ages?

9. Good examples of work coming from the sessions provide tangible evidence of what can be achieved and assist future staff discussion.

10. The sessions give a clear message to parents and to others of the intent of the school to take provision seriously.

However, enrichment sessions outside the normal classroom have to be seen as the icing on the cake.

KEY MESSAGE
Participation in enrichment sessions only accounts for a tiny part of all the work of the pupils. Delivery through normal lessons has to be seen overwhelmingly as the most important provision.

To extend the cake analogy, let's consider various scenarios:

1 No part of the cake has any substance
The main cake, the icing and the decoration are all poor – there is an absence of enrichment, extension, and differentiation, both inside and outside normal lessons.

2 **The decoration alone is real**
There are a few trimmings which give a superficial appearance of worth but neither normal lessons nor activities beyond have any real substance.

3 **The icing is good but not the cake beneath**
There are some good enrichment activities but they are 'bolted-on' to a poor basic curriculum pattern. The net effect is small and it is ruined by the bulk of what happens.

4 **The basic cake is good but there is no icing and there are no decorations**
Normal classroom activity involves enrichment and differentiation. Able pupils are well catered for but their appetite could be satisfied more fully with the addition of some special events and activities.

5 **All the parts of the cake not only look good but they are of good quality**
Here is the ideal product. Normal lessons cater well for able pupils who also benefit from additional activities. The decorations – certificates and the like – put the finishing touches to an excellent provision.

Some examples of enrichment activities

On the basis that understanding general principles is best achieved through specific examples, there follow the descriptions of various enrichment sessions which have been found to be successful. These are intended to give a general idea of the types of activities that can be included rather than to be taken as actual examples to try in the classroom.

Words are magic; words are fun

Target audience: 50 pupils from years Seven, Eight and Nine.

Selection process: Nomination by English staff on the basis of which children would derive the most benefit from the activities planned.

Timing: $3^1/_4$ hours morning session with a break of fifteen minutes.

Programme

1. Three 'warm-up' word games from **'Everyman's Word Games'** by Gyles Brandreth *(Dent, 1986)*:
   a) Peculiar Leader
   b) Follow On
   c) Coffee Pot

2. 'Silhouette' – an exercise designed by the author to examine the derivation of words and to classify them in groups. The piece of work entails the use of really good dictionaries.

3. The pupils followed a process of...
   a) choosing a verb
   b) finding a pun
   c) creating a sentence

   ...to produce 'Tom Swifties' in which the aim is to make up a pun on an adverb or adverbial phrase, e.g.:

"I got the first three wrong," said Tom forthrightly.
"Pass the cards," said Tom ideally.

4. In the later stages of the morning pupils had a choice of activity:

a) 'Declensions', a game of word-play in which an adverb is distorted to the extreme - e.g.:

I am *convinced*. > You are *biased*. >They are *bigoted*.

b) 'Splitwords', a word puzzle involving clues similar to those in cryptic crosswords - e.g.:

Clue: 'An advantageous purchase comprising a solid rod and profit.'
Answer: Bargain.

c) 'Many a true word', an exercise on malapropisms, in which children had to find 20 words incorrectly used, and had to suggest which words should have been used instead.

d) Writing a politically correct bedtime story (after an introductory section from James Finn Garner's book **'Politically Correct Bedtime Stories'**, *[Souvenir, 1994])*

e) 'Simon drew it' – producing a picture and caption in the style of Dartmouth-based artist Simon Drew (after a short video extract and being shown examples of his work – **'joined up whiting'**, **'poultry in motion'** etc.)

Feedback and value
- Very positive parental reaction.
- A team-teaching opportunity that was helpful for professional development.
- Useful subsequent discussion on the selection of pupils and how much behaviour rather than ability had played a part.
- Some excellent examples of work.
- Valuable comments from the questionnaire filled in by participants. Many remarked on the considerable enjoyment of the session, and many also expressed their appreciation of the challenge involved and of working with others who enjoy English. There were mixed views on the range of ages of pupils involved.

Other examples of enrichment activities
The following suggestions are offered to help your thinking and planning.

Competitions
Competitions are ready-made activities that you can tap into without too much preparation of your own. There are national competitions for many subject areas – in Mathematics, for example, national competitions are run by The Mathematics Association. A week rarely goes by without information in the school mail about competitions involving poetry or business studies, the environment, design, art etc..

Below are two ideas for competitions devised by the author, which could be run as enrichment activities for a class or a school.

'The Geography Person'

Task: Many place names have parts of the human body included in them, or sound like parts of the human body (e.g. Nor<u>thumb</u>erland, Abe<u>ryst</u>wyth). Write a list of actual geographical locations in Great Britain which suggest parts of the human body. You are encouraged to use your sense of humour by using puns and word play, but remaining 'decent'.

Judging: Entries will be assessed on the basis of the number and quality of the answers, including accuracy, technical detail and word play.

Advice: You may wish to research the human body and Great Britain.

Purpose: The competition combines Biology, Geography and English in a fun exercise.

A few answers from the many possible: Chester, Liverpool, Braintree, Exmouth, Trevose Head, Noseley, Heart's Delight, Kyle of Tongue, and also – St. Pancr(e)as Station, Middle Wallop, Musselburgh.

'Goldilocks'

This was aimed at Year 12 but it could be directed at different ages.

Activity: Write the closing speeches for the prosecution and defence at the trial of Goldilocks. You may wish:

    a) To research the story of **'Goldilocks and the Three Bears'**.
    b) To research the processes of law.
    c) To include ideas from many sources including philosophy, politics, law etc.
    d) To make good use of your imagination and your sense of humour.

What you can expect: Extremely witty, imaginative and word-rich answers such as these extracts from the defence statement of the winning entry:

"The prosecution claims to be blindfolded by the truth, though it appears that prejudice is the real blindfolder. Our esteemed friend calls white females 'the scourge of today's society.' This bias is merely a response to the racist dross spooled out by the media."

"We cannot take the testimony of Hank the woodsmith to be true for example. Hank is the fifth in a family of five sons, the typical attention seeker. His statement is merely a vain attempt for recognition amongst his family."

(Developed from an idea by Doug Ross.)

KEY MESSAGE

Go beyond the normal instructions into more unusual areas and you will open the door to imaginative responses full of individual ideas and creativity.

Activities within Local Education Authorities or 'clusters'

For schools within a local authority context there may well be activities which are open to pupils from a number of schools.

Devon LEA for example has organised:

> *residential and other events designed to draw together pupils with particular ability or talents and to provide them with specialised teaching designed to extend those abilities. There has been work of this nature in a number of fields including Mathematics, Computers, Modern Foreign Languages, Music, Science, Drama, Art and Physical Education.*

'A Devon Approach to Able And Talented Pupils', *(Devon County Council, 1992)*

Work in the Humanities area has developed since. For example:

- 'Small Town.....Big Decisions'. A Geography enrichment day organised by the subject adviser and the Associate Adviser for Able and Talented Pupils involving an enquiry and decision-making exercise based on Tiverton town centre.

- Chris Taylor, County Adviser for Humanities has developed work based upon Montacute House in Somerset. *"The aim was to make the activities genuinely challenging and lead to a piece of extended writing about rank and status in Elizabethan England."*

Schools not working within an LEA could explore the possibilities of 'buying-in' or working together in clusters where such a plan is geographically feasible.

KEY MESSAGE

Take advantage of area-based enrichment activities whether within the LEA or cluster organisation. Your share of organisation is limited to a reasonable level and your pupils meet and work with talented youngsters from other schools.

Activities organised by other agencies

<u>Universities</u>
- Masterclasses are run in many areas. Mathematics is particularly strongly supported in this way.
- LEA personnel can often 'broker' deals between a group of schools and individual university departments.
- Universities will sometimes provide students to work alongside school staff.
- Less familiar curriculum areas can be supported through universities, e.g. a Saturday morning Russian Club for 13-15 year-olds.

Residential centres

You will need to explore the field in your own locality. Below are two examples of centres in South-West England and one in Scotland.

- Longlands, Bovey Tracey, Devon, provide extension activities with the pupils working in small groups to solve difficult problems and tackle initiative tests that are used also for management training courses. Each group is carefully monitored and constantly put under the pressure of time limits and penalty points.
- Kilve Court, Somerset, runs a wide range of enrichment courses for able children of various ages across the curriculum.
- Aganippe, Banffshire, Scotland, is an educational trust established to provide specific provision for children of recognised or latent ability who are not achieving their potential. Courses *"are specifically designed to stimulate and develop children's abilities. The work will be fun but demanding and productive."* Although Aganippe is based in Scotland, a number of locations are used, including Hertfordshire, Machynlleth in mid-Wales, and West Sussex as well as Aberdeen, Perthshire and the Highlands.

Freelance individuals and organisations

There are many. Here are just a few examples. Addresses can be found on page 101.

- Scott Hurd provides a range of activities for Education and Industry. One particular service is Challenge Plus! *"extending, challenging and motivating young people of potential."*

  "Challenge Plus gives the most able students the opportunity to work in small, mixed teams to complete challenges and solve problems with tight deadlines in order to develop understanding and confidence in self and others. This well proven combination of brainstorming, challenge and simulated real-world activity, usually with industrial involvement, helps to develop each young person's awareness of themselves and the world that they will inherit."

  "Aims:
  - *to make students aware of their potential and responsibilities*
  - *to raise standards, giving students direction and purpose*
  - *to boost confidence in self and others*
  - *to improve communication and other skills necessary for teamwork*
  - *to have an enjoyable day"*

- GIFT offers a range of consultancy services but also a programme of individually-designed packages of curriculum enrichment. Some of these are residential (Years 5-13). Some examples are:

  'Twinkle Twinkle' – *"what is a star? Why do they shine?"*
  'The Longest Day' – *"a look at the events of June 6th 1944 with an eye to some of the problems faced by those who had to prepare."*
  'Genealogy' – *"a chance to explore a real family tree using original materials."*

  There are also many day courses, often run as Saturday masterclasses. Examples are:

  'Mirror Mirror' (Years 1/2) – *"reflecting upon the way mirrors work."*
  'Frankenstein' (Years 3/4) – *"a day of history, drama, literature and, of course, horror!"*

Effective Provision for Able & Talented Children

'A note to remember' (Years 5/6) – "*An opportunity for extended composition in music and for performance.*"

- The National Association for Gifted Children (NAGC) has Explorers' Clubs which "*provide stimulating and enriching activities in a friendly and supportive atmosphere. In small groups, children can pursue, with expert and enthusiastic adults, subjects which interest them. At the same time, they can interact with children of similar abilities and outlook.*"

- Mensa Foundation for Gifted Children organises Saturday schools and summer schools. "*We aim to provide stimulating companionship and enjoyable intellectual challenges.*" Events have included 'Bright Sparks' weekends in Scotland, Junior Mensa at Cambridge, and competitions through the regular magazine such as Junior Innovators.

KEY MESSAGE

Explore what is available in your locality and then take advantage of the opportunities that interest you most. If your area is less well served there are many ideas above, which you may wish to develop individually or collectively.

School-based activities

Below are some suggestions for enrichment activities that can be used within the school for the benefit of many pupils.

- A school newspaper organised and produced by the pupils themselves.
- A subject-based magazine in Mathematics, Science, History etc.
- Curriculum activities over an extended time period, perhaps of a more unusual nature, during an activities week for example. Murals, landscape painting, lace-making, the production of short videos, environmental projects, board games, costume design and a host of other activities are possible.
- Clubs at lunchtime or after school involving the non-standard activities of curriculum areas.
- Inter-form, inter-year, inter-house quizzes and competitions of every shape and size.
- Detailed investigations from 'one-liners'. Schools could emulate The Cleveland Science Project which used to stimulate exciting enrichment activities in their summer schools from such simple starting points as 'Why do moles inhabit some areas and not others?', and 'Is there a relationship between limpet size and their grazing area?'
- 'Feature days' or festivals celebrating the work of the particular curriculum area.
- The use of differentiated homeworks within an Individual Education Plan. (e.g. A pupil spending a great deal of time writing poetry and stories may well have such activities built into their homework in place of some tasks that might not be so beneficial.)
- A mentoring scheme which pairs an adult from within the school or from the wider community with a pupil, to share a common area of expertise, ability and interest.

You could also dedicate a section of the school library to the purchase and collection of enrichment materials, which are then available to pupils in the same way as other books.

KEY MESSAGE
Enrichment opportunities abound. By using a variety of methods, both within the school and outside, effective provision for able and talented children can be greatly enhanced.

In conclusion

- ☞ Normal classroom activity provides the great majority of what able pupils receive and, as such, it must be of high quality.

- ☞ Enrichment activities do, however, have a role.

- ☞ Some enrichment activities provide good opportunities for pupils of all abilities but there is also a strong need for sessions in which only able children take part.

- ☞ Enrichment activities encourage the use of high order thinking skills and they also match many of the characteristics of able children such as the capacity to work in the abstract, the love of word humour and the ability to see unusual connections.

- ☞ By taking advantage of the varied range of possible activities both inside school and beyond, able children's lives can be greatly enriched.

Section Eight

Monitoring and evaluation

This section will examine:

➡ how value added applies to able and talented pupils

➡ the concept of pupil evidence

➡ why monitoring and evaluation should take place

➡ who should be involved

➡ what areas should be monitored and evaluated

➡ what results should come out of the process

Value added

Many people are familiar with the notion of value added – i.e. measuring what a child can do at different points in time to see what improvements have been made. It might involve progress from the end of Key Stage 1 to the end of Key Stage 2 or the value added from GCSE to Advanced level. David Jesson of Sheffield University, and others, are developing the notion of a longitudinal view of value added from pre-school right through education, with a number of points of comparison along the way.

When a child starts from a low base it is reasonably easy to note the progress that he or she has made. However, a very able pupil soon reaches a good level of attainment, well ahead of chronological age. As output is of a good standard (unless the child is able but underachieving badly) lack of sufficient progress could well be missed. Yet value added is just as important in the education of the able and talented as it is for other children.

The longitudinal view of ability promoted by the work of people like David Jesson is also of value in the identification of able pupils and the provision for them.

Pupil evidence

A whole school policy backed by departmental policies provides a platform for development but the key question is whether individual pupils benefit from the policies in real terms. The gathering of pupil evidence supports, or otherwise, the effectiveness of the policies. For example, is there evidence of:

- pupils missing out a year?
- acceleration in a particular subject?
- involvement with groups outside school?
- individual timetables tailored to suit specific situations?
- entry into an examination not normally followed by the main group, e.g. Astronomy?
- pupils in older year groupings for a particular curriculum area?
- pupils with a good balance of teacher attention and independence of study?

Why monitor and evaluate?

1. If effective provision is the aim then it is what actually happens that counts, not what is hoped will happen.
2. To generate confidence in the policies.
3. To improve the procedures involved.
4. To strengthen any weak areas.
5. To inform future planning and action.

Who should be involved?

1. The pupils themselves – this is especially true of able and talented children.
2. Their parents and guardians who can assess the pastoral as well as the curricular effects.
3. The departments involved with the pupils.
4. The Able and Talented Pupils Co-ordinator.
5. The person responsible for monitoring and evaluation more generally in the school.
6. People to represent an 'external' view – perhaps advisers or consultants who have a broad picture of a number of schools.

What should be monitored and evaluated?

Monitoring is required to ensure that things actually happen, for example:

- Whole school policies are implemented
- Departmental policies are put into practice
- Homework is differentiated
- Grouping arrangements take place as planned
- Review dates within Individual Education Plans take place as scheduled
- Year Seven work does not involve unnecessary repetition (as there have been concerns that pupils in their first year at secondary school duplicate too much work that has been covered at the primary stage).

Evaluation is needed to judge how successfully things are operating, for example:

- How effective are the policies?
- Do pupils feel sufficiently challenged?
- Are pastoral arrangements giving pupils the necessary support?
- Do the Individual Education Plans work well to answer the needs of the pupils?
- Are staff confident about their ability to identify, and provide for, able and talented pupils?
- Is the weight of pupil evidence strong enough to indicate success of particular schemes?
- Has the concept of value added been met?

Checklist for schools/departments on able and talented pupils

The following checklist could be modified to suit particular schools (of differing phase, size etc.) and their stage of development. Although it has been written with provision for the able and talented in mind, it is relevant to the needs of many other pupils too.

1. Is there a whole school policy in operation?

2. Is there a named Co-ordinator for Able and Talented pupils? Do parents know who he / she is?

3. Is there a departmental policy?

4. Are the contents fully appreciated by all members of the department?

5. Have Inservice needs been met?

6. If not, what plans are there to answer the staff development needs?

7. Has the principle of differentiation been included clearly within departmental documentation, especially in work schemes?

8. How far are you satisfied that normal lesson delivery involves the full-time allocation of pace, urgency, drive and challenge for all the pupils, including the most able?

9. In terms of grouping policy -
   a) Where you use setting, are you satisfying the requirements detailed in the Able and Talented Pupils Policy?
   b) Where you are using mixed ability groups, are you satisfied that all abilities are being catered for, including the most able?

10. Have you written your own version of the Exceptional Performance Paragraph of the National Curriculum?

11. Have you drawn up a subject checklist and is it being used?

12. Do comments from parents, including feedback at parents evenings, convince you that they are happy that able children are being stretched and challenged?

13. Which special events and enrichment sessions have you run or are you going to run?

14. Is the department using a varied collection of resources and methods which goes beyond the 'standard texts'? What are they? Do they require varying periods of time?

15. Which subject-based competitions have you encouraged pupils to enter?

16. Which LEA activities do you take advantage of to broaden provision?

17. Which other activities outside school have been part of the department's provision?

18. Have you been able to utilise the local community either generally or as mentors/partners for pupils with particular interests?

19. Are you using differentiated homeworks?

20. Have you been involved in 'cluster' activities with other schools?

21. To what extent have links with national associations been helpful in provision for able pupils?

22. What strategies has the department agreed on, to deal with the situation when children finish work early (and well)?

23. What factors make a task or piece of work difficult or very challenging in your subject area? How have these factors been incorporated into departmental planning?

24. In what ways does the assessment policy of the department reflect the nature of ability in the particular subject and give credit for the unexpected but excellent response made by able pupils?

25. How does the department contribute to the school ethos in encouraging achievement and preventing underachievement caused by peer pressure?

26. Are rewards and sanctions applied fairly to take account of particular situations involving able pupils?

27. Is the department satisfied that there is a smooth transition from Year Six to Year Seven and that there is no unnecessary repetition?

28. Does the department have case studies which are helpful for professional development purposes?

29. Does the department collect and keep particular pieces of work of high quality to facilitate discussion and to help with Inservice training?

30. Is the department content that in its planning and delivery, the needs of able pupils are being met?

31. Do all the members of the department understand their role in filling out pupil referral sheets and contributing to Individual Education Plans?

32. What is the pupil evidence to support your answers to the above questions and any acceleration or individually-constructed programmes of work which have taken place?

This school/department checklist also provides a useful summary of the most important points in this book and, as such, is a checklist for the reader in his/her understanding of its contents.

The next stage

As part of a cyclical process the findings from monitoring and evaluation should have an impact on future plans and actions, and result in schools:

- taking remedial action where gaps are discovered
- amending policies to make provision more effective
- streamlining procedures where problems have occurred
- cutting out unnecessary paperwork without damaging the process
- providing Inservice work where lack of understanding is discovered
- taking account of changed circumstances, locally and nationally

And so......we continue to improve the effectiveness of provision for able and talented children.

In conclusion

- ☞ Policies and procedures need to be monitored and evaluated on a regular basis, to allow for necessary improvements which benefit the pupils through even more effective provision.

- ☞ Monitoring and evaluation should take place at an institutional level to see that policies and schemes operate in a general way, but also at a personal level to make sure that individual children are progressing properly.

- ☞ This personal level involves value added, Individual Education Plans and reviews of individual pupils.

- ☞ A checklist for departments and curriculum areas helps those in charge of particular areas to assess how well they are doing.

Resources

In this section you will see that:

➡ human resource is the most important for able children, as for all children

➡ financial resource allows discrete expenditure on enrichment activities and other forms of provision and also helps to give status and credibility to the issue of provision for the able and talented

➡ there are underlying curriculum principles to the needs of able and talented children and, with these in mind, material resources of all shapes and sizes can be used effectively and with benefit

Personnel

People are more important than anything else. The role of the classroom teacher is the most vital part of effective provision – for children of all abilities. The teacher can, and should , be supported by others. A Co-ordinator for Able and Talented Pupils has a key role to play. Section Five dealt fully with Personnel issues, and the role of the teacher in the classroom was further developed in Section Six.

Finance

An argument has already been advanced (see Section Five) for the creation of an enrichment budget line. It has several useful functions. However we must not fall into the trap of believing that spending power itself is the answer. This section will show that many existing materials can be put to good effect providing that the underlying curriculum principles are understood. Even so, some financial resource can act as a catalyst and a motivator.

Materials abound

There is little use in looking for and choosing resources unless you have clear in your mind what is needed. A series of steps are required:

1. Research curriculum principles and theory.
2. Establish a list of curriculum principles and ideas to underpin policy in the school.
3. Carry out an audit of existing materials.
4. Match the stock to the principles.
5. Amend the use of existing stock to answer the curriculum principles.
6. Plan how to make good important gaps in existing resources.

Before going on to look at particular resources available, it is important to acknowledge that many able children defy chronological age in terms of their development and capabilities. As a result it is very difficult and possibly misleading, to indicate specific ages for materials – unless they have been designed for a particular Key Stage. Some seven year-old children can undertake tasks successfully which many 14 year-olds would not be able to complete.

◆ Specifically produced materials

In this country not too many texts and materials are produced which are aimed specifically at the most able. This is for commercial reasons. Publishers prefer to market texts with a wider base so that sales are high.

Some standard texts have tried to meet the need by including enrichment and extension sections at the end of chapters. This is helpful and such sections often provide useful work (e.g. **'Understanding Mathematics'**, *C J Cox & D Bell [John Murray]).* However, on their own they cannot be said to deal fully with the needs of able pupils.

Materials deliberately produced for able and talented pupils include:
'Enrichment Activities for More Able Students', *D George & K Hughes (The Chalkface Project, for Key Stage 4, 1995)*
'Enrichment Activities for More Able Students 2', *J Morton & L Fabry (The Chalkface Project, for Key Stage 3, 1996)*
'Aquila' – *"The magazine for children who enjoy challenges."* This is a monthly publication aimed at children aged 8-13 (address on p.101)
'Bright Challenge', *R Casey & V Koshy (Stanley Thornes, 1995),* aimed at 7-11 year-olds. Able Children (address on p.101) have a range of materials for Key Stage 1 and 2. Amongst them are the Lancashire Primary Enrichment Materials and Extension Materials for Mathematically Able and Gifted Pupils. For Key Stage 3 there are cross-curriculum resource packs involving economic and industrial understanding.

It is worth noting that texts aimed at able children are much more readily available in the United States.

◆ Writing your own materials

There are advantages in approaching the task of making suitable resources available in this way. For example, the materials can be designed for specific use in the particular school. And, having spent time and effort, the teachers have a sense of ownership, which is more likely to lead to the use of what has been produced. There is also a very valuable professional development factor. Going through the thought processes to write suitable enrichment and extension materials is a productive and effective form of Inservice work. However, on the downside, a large amount of time is required – and teachers seem to come under more pressures every year that goes by.

If you do want to write your own materials the first step is to decide upon the curriculum principles involved, the target group, and whether they will slot into a subject area or be cross-curricular. It is helpful to have some books which are the 'raw materials' – books that contain interesting ideas which can provide the starting point. Here are some examples:

'Second Best Bed', *Fenton Bresler (Weidenfeld and Nicolson, 1983).* This is an amusing book tracing the story of wills and their sometimes baffling legal complexities. It could be used for activities to encourage precision in language.

'**Is Heathcliff A Murderer?**', *John Sutherland (Oxford University Press, 1996)*. This contains investigations of 34 conundrums of nineteenth century fiction, which are useful for encouraging children to reach their own conclusions by studying evidence and solving mysteries.

An alternative is to adapt materials for your own use. This is a 'half-way house' between using existing materials and writing your own. Some of the materials suitable for adaptation might not be commercially produced by a large publishing company but may be available from LEA groups or individual authors. In this case the work can be used as 'exemplar materials' which stimulate further development. Authors are usually pleased to see original materials taken on and amended for new purposes.

◆　**Children's literature**

Reading for pleasure and personal development remains a key activity for all children, not just the most able. We live in an increasingly visual world which offers many opportunities but which also has some dangers. In reading, as in other activities, progression is a key consideration.

Veronica Jones and Annie James, the library assistants at The King's School, Ottery St. Mary, have prepared a 'Recommended Reading for Able Readers' list. This would be valuable in all secondary schools.

> *"The booklist is graded from 1-4 according to the complexity and accessibility of the themes explored therein. These include moral issues, relationships, bereavement, family breakdown, race and gender issues, group pressure, disability, war and the use and misuse of power."*

> *"Students are encouraged to read from this list as they become confident and able readers, and to progress from level 1 to 4 through years 7, 8 and 9. They are also encouraged to make their own suggestions as to suitable books which might be added to the list."*

Similarly, a primary school could construct an appropriate list for progression through Key Stages 1 and 2.

◆　**Resources for Mathematics**

This is perhaps the subject area that frightens more people than any other and yet it is the one best served by wonderful enrichment material. Brian Bolt, David Wells, Martin Gardner, Lewis Carroll and many others have served up a feast of magic and excitement. One chapter of Roy Kennard's **'Teaching Mathematically Able Children'** *(NACE/DfEE, 1996)* has many suggestions. He says,

The intention behind the compilation of resources is to provide teachers with a starting point rather than an exhaustive list.

Here are just a few useful titles:

● 　The following by Brian Bolt *(Cambridge University Press)*:
　　　'Mathematical Activities' *(1982)*
　　　'The Amazing Mathematical Amusement Arcade' *(1984)*
　　　'More Mathematical Activities' *(1985)*
　　　'Even More Mathematical Activities' *(1987)*
　　　'Mathematical Funfair' *(1989)*
　　　'101 Mathematical Projects' (with David Hobbs, *1989)*

- Russian mathematicians are involved with exciting materials:
  'The Chicken from Minsk', *Y Chernyak & R Rose (Weidenfeld and Nicolson, 1996).*
  'The Moscow Puzzles', *Boris Kordemsky (Penguin, 1976)*
  'The Psychology of Mathematical Abilities in Schoolchildren', *V A Krutetskii (University of Chicago Press, 1976)*

- The following titles by Martin Gardner, *(Penguin)*:
  'Mathematical Puzzles and Diversions' *(1965)*
  'Further Mathematical Diversions' *(1977)*
  'Mathematical Circus' *(1981)*

- Dover Publications have published some excellent titles including:
  'The Canterbury Tales', *H E Dudeney (1958)*
  'Entertaining Mathematical Puzzles', *Martin Gardner (1986)*
  'Mathematics, Magic and Mystery', *Martin Gardner (1956)*
  'Mathematical Puzzles of Sam Loyd', *Martin Gardner (ed.) (1959)*
  'Mathematical Brain-Teasers', *J A Hunter (1976)*
  'More Fun with Figures', *J A Hunter (1966)*
  'Tangrams 330 Puzzles', *Ronald C Read (1965)*
  'Lewis Carroll's Games and Puzzles', *Edward Wakeling (ed.) (1992)*
  'Rediscovered Lewis Carroll Puzzles', *Edward Wakeling (ed.) (1995)*

- The following titles by David Wells:
  'Can You Solve These?' Series 1,2 and 3 *(Tarquin, 1982, 1984, 1986)*
  'The Penguin Dictionary of Curious and Interesting Numbers', *(Penguin, 1986)*

- **'Flatland'**, *Edwin A Abbott (Penguin, 1986)*

- **'Board Games Around The World – a resource book for mathematical investigations'** *Bell & Cornelius (Cambridge University Press, 1988)*

◆ Games

Many games involve tactics and strategy. They are ideal vehicles for problem-solving, decision-making and creative thinking. Why are some moves and tactics successful and others unsuccessful? What would be the result of a change in the rules? Can you create your own game that works and challenges?

There are a number of games which provide good opportunities for analysis – go, mancala, chess, backgammon, brax. **'The Book of Classic Board Games'**, *Sid Sackson (Klutz Press, California, 1991)*, is one of many collections of such games. **'Dungeons and Dragons'** and other fantasy games have a huge following. There are also many books written about games or containing games in a book format, some of which are listed below:

'The Book of Games', *Peter Arnold (ed.), (Hamlyn, 1989)*
'The Winner's Guide to Games', *Gyles Brandreth (Guinness, 1992)*
'Darts', *Jabez Gotobed (The Oleander Press, 1980)*
'The Gamut of Games', *Sid Sackson (Dover Publications, 1992)*
'The Chess Mysteries of Sherlock Holmes', *Raymond Smullyan (Hutchinson, 1980)*

'The Chess Mysteries of the Arabian Knights', *Raymond Smullyan (Hutchinson, 1983)*
'Pick a Pair!', *F Tapson & A Parr (A & C Black, 1979)*
'Take Two!', *Frank Tapson (A & C Black, 1977)*
'Dice Games New and Old', *William E Tredd (The Oleander Press, 1981)*

There is a huge array of computer games. Many children, including the most able, derive great pleasure and benefit from them. What they can miss are the social advantages of playing games in company.

◆ **Detective materials**

Logical thought, deductive reasoning and problem-solving are represented strongly in detective materials. Many pupils regard the content as interesting and entertaining (as do many adults). Combining skills and concepts with an interesting vehicle makes for good education and strong motivation.

Just a few titles as examples:
'The Eleventh Hour', *Graeme Base (Puffin, 1993)*
'Almost Perfect Crimes', *Hy Conrad (Sterling, 1995)*
'The Book of Clues', *John Sladek (Corgi, 1984)*
'Cluedo Armchair Detective', *Lawrence Treat (Dorling Kindersley, 1983)*

◆ **Mysteries**

Most people are intrigued by happenings that are difficult to explain. This is certainly true of able children. Profitable work can be done on unsolved mysteries and on the reasons behind dramatic events. Able pupils in Saturday Clubs or other activities have shown no reticence in finding solutions to situations that have baffled the world for centuries!

The Marie Celeste, Devon Loch, spontaneous combustion, the Bermuda Triangle, UFO's, Atlantis – these and many more make very suitable subjects for activities. **'The Reader's Digest Book of Strange Stories, Amazing Facts'** *(Reader's Digest, 1981)*, contains a good section on intriguing and unsolved mysteries.

◆ **Codes**

Codes, particularly difficult examples, are ideal material around which to design activities for the able and talented, for the following reasons:

- They provide a real challenge. Many able pupils succeed too easily and do not struggle enough. This is damaging for their personal development.
- They have an abstract quality which suits the able. Piaget talked of leading children from the concrete to the abstract. Many able pupils can go straight to the abstract.
- They answer some of the requirements in the Mathematics orders of the National Curriculum.
- They stimulate good working methods as the attempted solutions to codes need careful recording or the code-breaker goes round in circles.

Three titles to look out for:

> **'Mr. Enigma's Code Mysteries'**, *Tom Healey (Beaver, 1982)*
> **'Games with Codes and Ciphers'**, *Norvin Pallas (Dover Publications, 1994)*
> **'Cryptography: the science of secret writing'**, *Laurence Dwight Smith (Dover Publications, 1955)*

It is also very worthwhile to get children to write their own codes, at differing levels of difficulty.

◆ Treasure hunts

'Treasure Hunt' has been a popular television programme. In recent years there has also been the growth of books with complicated texts and splendid illustrations which allow the reader to trace treasure in one form or another. Vocabulary skills and deductive reasoning are required. Here is a list of some of the texts:

> **'The Piper of Dreams'**, *Terry Pitts Fenby (Hodder and Stoughton, 1982)*
> **'Treasure'**, *Dan James (Ordnance Survey, 1994)*
> **'Conundrum'**, *Don Shaw (Hamlyn, 1984)*
> **'Masquerade'**, *Kit Williams (Jonathan Cape, 1979)*
> **'Quest for the Golden Hare'**, *Bamber Gascoigne (Jonathan Cape, 1983)* includes a description of the solutions to Williams', **'Masquerade'**
> The bee book, where the challenge was to discover the title!, *Kit Williams, (Jonathan Cape, 1984)*

◆ Word games, word power, word play

Checklists of characteristics associated with able children often include enjoyment of puns, nuances and double meanings, a fascination with the derivation and the use of words and a particular sense of humour (the 'off-the-wall' or 'quirky'). Creative and imaginative work abounds in this area which is well served by a wealth of material. Here are some examples:

> **'The Oxford Guide to Word Games'**, *Tony Augarde (Oxford University Press, 1986)*
> **'Animalia'**, *Graeme Base (Puffin, 1990)*
> **'Everyman's Word Games'**, *Gyles Brandreth (Dent, 1986)*
> **'Handel's Warthog Music'**, *Simon Drew (Antique Collector's Club, 1993)*
> **'Beastly Address Book'**, *Simon Drew, (Antique Collector's Club, 1993)*
> **'Beastly Birthday Book'**, *Simon Drew, (Antique Collector's Club, 1995)*
> **'Politically Correct Bedtime Stories'**, *James Finn Garner (Souvenir Press, 1994)*
> **'Once Upon a More Enlightened Time'**, *James Finn Garner (Simon & Schuster, 1995)*
> **'Professor Branestawm's Dictionary'**, *Norman Hunter (Puffin, 1973)*
> **'Spooner or Later'**, *P Jennings, T Greenwood & T Denton (Viking, 1992)*
> **'The Play of Words'**, *Richard Lederer (Pocket Books, 1990)*
> **'The Penguin Book of Word Games'**, *David Parlett (Penguin, 1982)*
> **'The Ultimate Alphabet'**, *Mike Wilks (Pavilion, 1986)*

◆ Thinking skills

Is there a need for a specific course on thinking skills to underpin the curriculum or should these skills be embedded in the subject area? Fuerstein's 'Instrumental Enrichment' programme has been linked with provision for backward children but the abstract quality of the exercises not only makes them relatively content free but also allows open-ended responses. A fairly recent publication by Howard Sharron and

Martha Coulter, **'Changing Children's Minds'** *(Imaginative Minds, 1994)*, explores the course and its uses.

It was work on Instrumental Enrichment which led to further development in Somerset. Nigel Blagg, Marj Ballinger and Richard Gardner have produced several modules of the **'Somerset Thinking Skills Course'** *(Basil Blackwell in association with Somerset County Council, 1988)*:

Module 1:   Foundations for problem solving
Module 2:   Analysing and synthesising
Module 3:   Comparative thinking
Module 4:   Positions in time and space
Module 5:   Understanding analogies
Module 6:   Patterns in time and space
Module 7:   Organising and memorising

Matthew Lipman, an American philosopher, created a programme called 'Philosophy for Children'. He decided to use narratives as a way into exploration of philosophical ideas with children. Now Dr. Richard Fox, a lecturer in Primary Education at the University of Exeter, has written **'Thinking Matters: Stories to Encourage Thinking Skills'**, *(Southgate, 1996)*. The book is aimed at pupils in Years 5 and 6 and the work is deliberately linked to the National Curriculum. The stories do however have relevance for children in the early years of secondary school.

Edward de Bono has an international reputation for thinking skills techniques and materials. Penguin Books have published a number of his texts:

'The Five-day Course in Thinking' *(1969)*
'The Use of Lateral Thinking' *(1971)*
'The Dog-Exercising Machine' *(1971)*
'Po: Beyond Yes and No' *(1972)*
'Children Solve Problems' *(1972)*
'Practical Thinking' *(1976)*
'Teaching Thinking' *(1978)*

Dorling Kindersley in 1995 published Edward de Bono's **'Mind Pack'** in which he *"takes familiar ideas and associations and redefines them to make everyday thinking enjoyable."* The pack includes a 72-page guide to more than 80 thinking games and exercises.

◆   <u>Science</u>
The revised version of the National Curriculum devotes 57 pages to Science, far more than any other subject (e.g.s: English - 31 pages; Mathematics - 30 pages). Content description takes up a great deal of the space. Perhaps then we should be on the lookout particularly for books and materials which explore the higher order thinking skills and/or enjoyment. Some suggestions:

'Entertaining Science Experiments with Everyday Objects' *Martin Gardner (Dover Publications, 1981)*
'The Flying Circus of Physics', *Jearl Walker (John Wiley & Sons, 1975)*
'Tricks with Science, Words and Numbers', *Alan Ward (Batsford, 1983)*
'The Ultimate Noah's Ark', *Mike Wilks (Michael Joseph, 1993)*

◆ <u>**Puzzles and brainteasers of many kinds**</u>

Much of what many practitioners use does not come from standard textbooks. The materials used are the result of an open mind as to what do constitute suitable curriculum resources for the able and talented. There is a wealth of material in puzzles and brainteasers which provides challenge, breadth and enjoyment – essential ingredients in a curriculum for the able.

Some of the sections above have already described items which would fit this category – word puzzles, detective exercises, mathematical puzzles etc. Here is just a short selection from a vast list of what is available:

- Mensa produces a great deal of its own material:
  'The Ultimate Mental Challenge', *Robert Allen (Carlton, 1995)*
  'Riddles and Conundrums', *Robert Allen (Carlton, 1995)*
  'Logic Puzzles', *Robert Allen (Carlton, 1996)*
  'The IQ Challenge', *Philip Carter and Ken Russell (Greenwich Editions, 1994)*
  'Boost Your IQ' *H Gale & C Skitt (Carlton, 1994)*
  'A Mensa Puzzle Book', *Victor Serebriakoff (Muller, 1982)*

- Two unusual History resources:
  'Parallel Universe', *N Baxter & M Taylor (Franklin Watts, 1996)* – in each of 13 time zones, protected by a cyberform, you have to locate 20 misplaced objects.
  'The History Puzzle', *Cherry Denman, (Sinclair-Stevenson, 1994)* – over a thousand people to spot in the beautiful illustrations.

- Raymond Smullyan has earlier been listed for his two superb chess mysteries books. Also try:
  'What is the Name of this Book?' *(Penguin, 1981)*
  'The Lady or the Tiger?' *(Penguin, 1983)*
  'Alice in Puzzle-land' *(Penguin, 1984)*

- Lagoon Games have an attractive four-book set:
  'Classic Logic Puzzles' *(1994)*
  'Conundrums and Puzzles' *(1994)*
  'Classic Word Puzzles' *(1994)*
  'Lateral Thinking Puzzles' *(1994)*

- Now just a selection of others:
  'Everyman's Classic Puzzles', *Gyles Brandreth (Dent, 1985)*
  'Journey Through Puzzleland', *Erwin Brecher (Pan, 1994)*
  'The Sherlock Holmes IQ Book', *E Butler & M Pirie (Pan, 1995)*
  'Position the Poolballs Puzzle', *Cryptic Classics (Crystal Lines, 1993)*
  'Quiz Link', *Bill Murray (Helicon, 1995)*
  'Brainstormers Puzzle Book', *NACE, (NACE, 1996)*
  'The Celtic Knotwork Puzzle', *Past Times (Historical Collections, 1992)*
  'Lateral Thinking Puzzlers', *Paul Sloane (Sterling, 1992)*
  'The Ticket to Heaven', *Tim Sole (Penguin, 1988)*
  'The Sunday Times Book of Brainteasers', *Xerxes (ed.) (Times Books, 1994)*

◆ <u>**'Conversion materials'**</u>

This is a name made up to describe materials which can be used for enrichment work even though that was not their original use. Here are some examples of conversion materials that have been used successfully:

- A giant-sized red plastic pen which contained chocolate at Christmas time. This was used as a stimulus for creative writing. In this particular case you are playing with the notion of relative size and this is a key concept in many children's books ('**Gulliver's Travels'**, '**Alice in Wonderland'**, '**Jack and the Beanstalk'**). Many other objects could be used to stimulate imaginative writing – the imaginary contents from the jacket of a missing person, or a strange object whose function is not immediately clear, for instance.

- A sports firm sheet of many different coloured shirts in rows of 15, 11-deep, labelled 1-15 and A-K. This provides a perfect illustration upon which to set a logical thought problem. The co-ordinates could play a part in an order for shirts which have gone missing perhaps. From clues, the child has to reconstruct the original order. Alternatively, if accompanied by an instruction paper, the sheet could provide a colourful information sheet upon which to base a difficult code.

- Children's picture books and story books normally have wonderful illustrations and a text which is full of rhythm. Couple the young child's book with a list of figures of speech from an advanced text such as Chris Baldick's '**Oxford Concise Dictionary of Literary Terms'** *(Oxford University Press, 1991)*, and you can then ask older, able English pupils to find examples from the story books of: colloquialism, homonym, onomatopoeia, euphemism, irony, anachronism, alliteration, tragic flaw, poetic justice, personification etc.

- Different examples of wrapping paper can be used as conversion materials. Patterned papers lend themselves to Maths problems; one overall illustration suits observation work or creative writing – as the inspiration for a poem or a piece of prose perhaps.

The following example uses a sheet of wrapping paper showing various different images of sea life. Pupils are asked to produce a news item from the previous two years for each of the objects on the paper. These news items can refer either to the 'straight' name of the object or involve a play on words or a reference to the object's characteristics. For instance, an image of a plaice could be linked to a story about a 'place', an image of a shell could produce a news item about the oil company, a shrimp could bring to mind an item about a small person or faction, a crab might be connected with an item about a sideways move in someone's career... and so on.

This activity combines observation, current affairs and marine biology with word play and humour.

In conclusion

- ☞ Anything could be used as an enrichment resource once the curriculum principles and the needs of able and talented pupils are understood.

- ☞ "Enrichment is in the eye of the beholder."

If you have enjoyed reading this book, you may be interested to know about the sequel 'Effective Resource for Able and Talented Children' by the same author. Barry Teare in fact runs an extensive number of training events and conferences on the theme of able and talented children, which are very well received by his audiences. An outcome of the positive evaluations from the delegates at these events is that colleagues would like to be able to use the actual resources with which Barry Teare illustrates his talks. This second book is the result ....

Effective Resources for Able and Talented Children

This book contains a wide range of highly practical photocopiable resources for able and talented children in both the primary and secondary sectors. In effect it applies the strategies you have just been reading about and thus helps to really engage the children in the activities involved. It is full of activities that stretch and challenge children, encouraging them to display their true potential. It will let them shine!

'Effective Resources for Able and Talented Children' is broken down into National Curriculum areas with a foreword outlining the key principles. Curriculum areas covered include:

- Literacy
- Language across the curriculum
- Reading
- Writing
- Numeracy, Mathematics
- Science
- Logical Thought
- Codes
- Humanities
- Detective work

This book is available from the same publishers, Network Educational Press for £24.95 + £2.50 p&p

Network Educational Press Ltd., PO Box 635, Stafford, ST16 1BF
Tel: 01785 225515   Fax: 01785 228566
Email: enquiries@networkpress.co.uk
www.networkpress.co.uk

It will let them shine!

Bibliography

City of Birmingham, **'Gifted And Outstanding Children'**, 1978

DFE, **'The National Curriculum'**, HMSO, 1995

DfEE, **'Self-Government for Schools'**, HMSO, 1996

Department of National Heritage, **'Setting the Scene: The Arts and Young People'**, 1996

Department of National Heritage, **'Sport: Raising the Game'**, 1995

Department of National Heritage, **'Sport: Raising the Game, The First Year Report'**, 1996

Devon County Council, **'A Devon Approach to Able and Talented Pupils'**, 1992

Chris Dickinson, **'Effective Learning Activities'**, Network Educational Press, 1996

Patrick Dickinson, **'Could Do Better'**, Arrow Books, 1982

The Engineering Council, **'Engineering for People'**

Nicolas Evans, **'The Horse Whisperer'**, Corgi, 1994

Deborah Eyre, **'Able Children in Ordinary Schools'**, David Fulton, 1997

Deborah Eyre, **'School Governors and More Able Children'**, NACE/DfEE, 1995

Deborah Eyre & Tom Marjoram, **'Enriching and Extending The National Curriculum'**, Kogan Page, 1990

Joan Freeman, **'Gifted Children Growing Up'**, Cassell, 1991

Joan Freeman, **'The Psychology of Gifted Children'**, John Wiley & Sons Ltd., 1985

Howard Gardner, **'Frames Of Mind'**, Fontana, 1993

Martin Gardner, **'Further Mathematical Diversions'**, Penguin, 1969

David George, **'Gifted Education: Identification and Provision'**, David Fulton, 1995

Charles Handy, **'The Empty Raincoat'**, Hutchinson, 1994

HMI, **'The Education of Very Able Children in Maintained Schools'**, 1992

HMI, **'Gifted Children in Middle and Comprehensive Schools'**, HMSO, 1977

Hoyle and Wilks, **'Gifted Children and their Education'**, DES, 1974

Dr George Ilsley, **'Training the Teachers'**, NACE, 1991.

Roy Kennard, **'Teaching Mathematically Able Children'**, NACE/DfEE, 1996

V A Krutetskii, **'The Psychology of Mathematical Abilities in Schoolchildren'**, University of Chicago Press, 1976

Susan Leyden, **'Helping the Child of Exceptional Ability'**, Croom Helm, 1985

Dame Alicia Markova, **'Markova Remembers'**, Hamish Hamilton, 1986

Diane Montgomery, **'Educating the Able'**, Cassell, 1996

Margaret Morley, **'Larger Than Life'**, Robson Books, 1979

OFSTED **'A Review of Inspection Findings'**, HMSO, 1995

REACH, **'Primary Guidelines for Gifted and More Able Children'**, Solihull Metropolitan Borough Council

Anita Straker, **'Mathematics for Gifted Pupils'**, Longmans, 1983

J B Teare, **'Able Pupils: Practical Identification Strategies'**, NACE/DfEE, 2nd edition, 1996

J B Teare, **'A School Policy on Provision for Able Pupils'**, NACE/DfEE, 2nd edition, 1996

J B Teare, **'The King's School Policy for Able And Talented Pupils'**, 1992

Belle Wallace, **'Teaching the Very Able Child'**, Ward Lock Educational, 1983

The following publications are particularly useful:

'Official texts'

Hoyle and Wilks, **'Gifted Children and their Education'**, DES, 1974
HMI, **'Gifted Children in Middle and Comprehensive Secondary Schools'**, HMSO, 1977 (although old this is still a very valuable source)
HMI, **'The Education of Very Able Children in Maintained Schools'**, 1992
Deborah Eyre, **'School Governors and More Able Children'**, NACE/DfEE, 1995

Subject-based texts

Dr W H Cockcroft, **'Mathematics Counts'**, HMSO, 1981
Roy Kennard, **'Teaching Mathematically Able Children'**, NACE/DfEE, 1996
Anita Straker, **'Mathematics for Gifted Pupils'**, Longmans, 1983
HMI, **'Teaching Poetry in the Secondary School'**, HMSO, 1987
Assessment Performance Unit, **'How Well Can 15 Year-olds Write?'**, DES, 1983
UK Council for Music Education and Training, **'Musical Giftedness in the Primary School'**, Pullen Publications, 1982
Neville Grenyer, **'Geography for Gifted Pupils'**, Longmans, 1983

Good general texts

Deborah Eyre, **'Able Pupils in Ordinary Schools'**, David Fulton, 1997
David George, **'The Challenge of the Able Child'**, David Fulton, 1992
David George, **'Gifted Education: Identification and Provision'**, David Fulton 1995
Trevor Kerry, **'Finding and Helping the Able Child'**, Croom Helm, 1983
Tom Marjoram & Deborah Eyre, **'Enriching and Extending The National Curriculum'**, Kogan Page, 1990
Tom Marjoram, **'Able Children'**, Pullen Publications, 1995
Diane Montgomery, **'Educating the Able'**, Cassell, 1996.
J B Teare, **'A School Policy on Provision for Able Pupils'**, NACE/DfEE, 2nd edition 1996
J B Teare, **'Able Pupils: Practical Identification Strategies'**, NACE/DfEE, 2nd edition 1996
Belle Wallace, **'Teaching the Very Able Child'**, Ward Lock Educational, 1983
Peter Young & Colin Tyre, **'Gifted or Able?'**, Open University Press 1992

Good texts with an especially strong pastoral element

Joan Freeman, **'Gifted Children'**, MTP Press, 1979
Joan Freeman, **'Gifted Children Growing Up'**, Cassell 1991
Joan Freeman, Pieter Span & Harald Wagner, **'Actualising Talent'**, Cassell, 1995
Susan Leyden, **'Helping the Child of Exceptional Ability'**, Croom Helm, 1985
Frieda Painter, **'Living with a Gifted Child'**, Souvenir Press, 1984

'Linked' texts

B S Bloom, **'Developing Talent in Young People'**, Ballantine Books, 1985

C Dickinson & J Wright, **'Differentiation: A Practical Handbook of Classroom Strategies'**, NCET, 1993

Chris Dickinson, **'Effective Learning Activities'**, Network Educational Press, 1996

Howard Gardner, **'Frames of Mind'**, Fontana, 1993

Liam Hudson, **'Contrary Images'**, Penguin, 1967

NFER-Nelson, **'Educational Assessment: The Way Forward'**, NFER-Nelson, 1994

Alistair Smith, **'Accelerated Learning in the Classroom'**, Network Educational Press, 1996

J B Teare, **'Effective Resources for Able and Talented Children'**, Network Educational Press, 1999

K Urban and H Jellen, **'The Test for Creative Thinking'**, University of Hanover, 1988

USEFUL ADDRESSES

Able Children
Pullen Publications Ltd.
13 Station Road, KNEBWORTH, Herts, SG3 6AP

Aganippe
Educational Trust
Rosarie House, MULBEN, Keith, Banffshire, Scotland, AB55 3YU

Aquila Magazine
P.O. BOX 2518, Eastbourne, East Sussex, BN21 2BB

Association of Teachers of Mathematics Publications
7 Shaftesbury Street, DERBY, DE23 8YB

BAYS
British Asssociation for the Advancement of Science
23 Savile Row, LONDON, WIX 2NB

CREST Awards
CREST National Centre
1 Giltspur Street, LONDON, EC1A 9DD

European Council for High Ability (ECHA)
c/o Johanna Raffan, NACE, (Address below)

GIFT
The International Study Centre
Dartford Grammar School, WEST HILL, Dartford, Kent, DA1 2HW

Gwen Goodhew
The Able Child Centre
Calday Grammar School, WEST KIRBY, Wirral

Scott Hurd
Services for Education and Industry. Tel 01280 704962

Kilve Court Residential Education Centre
KILVE, Bridgwater, Somerset, TA5 1EA

Longlands
Environmental Field Study Centre for Residential Learning
HENNOCK, Bovey Tracey, Devon, TQ13 9QE

Mathematics Association
259 London Road, LEICESTER, LE2 3BE

Mensa Foundation for Gifted Children
Mensa House, St John's Square, WOLVERHAMPTON, WV2 4AH

National Association for Able Children in Education (NACE)
Westminster College, OXFORD, OX2 9AT

National Association for Gifted Children (NAGC)
National Centre for Children with High Abilities and Talents
Elder House, MILTON KEYNES, MK9 1LR

Network Educational Press Ltd.
Educational Publishing and Training
PO BOX 635, STAFFORD, ST16 1BF

Tarquin Publications
STRADBROKE, Diss, Norfolk, IP21 5JP

J B Teare
Education Consultant on Able and Talented Pupils
17 Durham Close, EXMOUTH, Devon, EX8 5QU

World Council for Gifted Children
210 Lindquist Center, The University of Iowa, IOWA CITY,
Iowa 52242 1529, USA

Effective Provison for Able & Talented Children is the seventh title in The School Effectiveness Series, which focuses on practical and useful ideas for school teachers. This series addresses the issues of whole school improvement, explores new knowledge about teaching and learning, and offers straightforward solutions which teachers can use to make life more rewarding for themselves and those they teach.

Book 1: *Accelerated Learning in the Classroom* by Alistair Smith
ISBN: 1855390345   £15.95

- The first book in the UK to apply new knowledge about the brain to classroom practice
- Contains practical methods so teachers can apply accelerated learning theories to their own classrooms
- Aims to increase the pace of learning and deepen understanding
- Includes advice on how to create the ideal environment for learning and how to help learners fulfil their potential
- Full of lively illustrations, diagrams and plans
- Offers practical solutions on improving performance, motivation and understanding
- Contains a checklist of action points for the classroom – 21 ways to improve learning

Book 2: *Effective Learning Activities* by Chris Dickinson
ISBN: 1855390353   £8.95

- An essential teaching guide which focuses on practical activities to improve learning
- Aims to improve results through effective learning, which will raise achievement, deepen understanding, promote self-esteem and improve motivation
- Includes activities which are designed to promote differentiation and understanding
- Offers advice on how to maximise the use of available – and limited – resources
- Includes activities suitable for GCSE, National Curriculum, Highers, GSVQ and GNVQ
- From the author of the highly acclaimed 'Differentiation: A Practical Handbook of Classroom Strategies'

Book 3: *Effective Heads of Department* by Phil Jones & Nick Sparks
ISBN: 1855390361   £8.95

- An ideal support for Heads of Department looking to develop necessary management skills
- Contains a range of practical systems and approaches; each of the eight sections ends with a 'checklist for action'
- Designed to develop practice in line with OFSTED expectations and DfEE thinking by monitoring and improving quality
- Addresses issues such as managing resources, leadership, learning, departmental planning and making assessment valuable
- Includes useful information for Senior Managers in schools who are looking to enhance the effectiveness of their Heads of Department

Book 4: *Lessons are for Learning* by Mike Hughes
ISBN: 1855390388   £11.95

- Brings together the theory of learning with the realities of the classroom environment
- Encourages teachers to reflect on their own classroom practice and challenges them to think about why they teach in the way they do
- Develops a clear picture of what constitutes effective classroom practice
- Offers practical suggestions for activities that bridge the gap between recent developments in the theory of learning and the constraints of classroom teaching
- Ideal for stimulating thought and generating discussion
- Written by a practising teacher who has also worked as a teaching advisor, a PGCE co-ordinator and an OFSTED inspector

Book 5: *Effective Learning in Science* by Paul Denley and Keith Bishop
ISBN: 1855390395   £11.95

- A new book that looks at planning for effective learning within the context of science
- Encourages discussion about the aims and purposes in teaching science and the role of subject knowledge in effective teaching
- Tackles issues such as planning for effective learning, the use of resources and other relevant management issues
- Offers help in the development of a departmental plan to revise schemes of work, resources classroom strategies, in order to make learning and teaching more effective
- Ideal for any science department aiming to increase performance and improve results

Book 6: *Raising Boys' Achievement* by Jon Pickering
ISBN: 185539040X   £11.95

- Addresses the causes of boys' underachievement and offers possible solutions
- Focuses the search for causes and solutions on teachers working in the classrooms
- Looks at examples of good practice in schools to help guide the planning and implementation of strategies to raise achievement
- Offers practical, 'real' solutions along with tried and tested training suggestions
- Ideal as a basis for INSET or as a guide to practical activities for classroom teachers

Book 8: *Effective Careers Education & Guidance* by Andrew Edwards and Anthony Barnes
ISBN: 1-85539-045-0   £11.95
- Strategic planning of the careers programme as part of the wider curriculum
- Practical consideration of managing careers education and guidance
- Practical activities for reflection and personal learning, and case studies where such activities have been used
- Aspects of guidance and counselling involved in helping students to understand their own capabilities and form career plans
- Strategies for reviewing and developing existing practice

Book 9: *Best behaviour and Best behaviour FIRST AID* by Peter Relf, Rod Hirst,
                                                    Jan Richardson and GeorginaYoudell

ISBN: 1-85539-046-9   £12.95
- Provides support for those who seek starting points for effective behaviour management, for individual teachers and for middle and senior managers
- Focuses on practical and useful ideas for individual schools and teachers

Best behaviour FIRST AID
ISBN: 1-85539-047-7   £10.50 (pack of 5 booklets)
- Provides strategies to cope with aggression, defiance and disturbance
- Straightforward action points for self-esteem

Book 10: *The Effective School Governor* by David Marriott
ISBN 1-85539-042-6   £15.95 (including free audio tape)
- Straightforward guidance on how to fulfil a governor's role and responsibilities
- Develops your personal effectiveness as an individual governor
- Practical support on how to be an effective member of the governing team
- Audio tape for use in car or at home

Book 11: *Improving Personal Effectiveness for Managers in Schools* by James Johnson
ISBN 1-85539-049-3   £11.95

- An invaluable resource for new and experienced teachers in both primary and secondary schools
- Contains practical strategies for improving leadership and management skills
- Focuses on self-management skills, managing difficult situations, working under pressure, developing confidence, creating a team ethos and communicating effectively

Book 12: *Making Pupil Data Powerful* by Maggie Pringle and Tony Cobb
ISBN 1-85539-052-3   £12.95

- Shows teachers in primary, middle and secondary schools how to interpret pupils' performance data and how to use it to enhance teaching and learning
- Provides practical advice on analysing performance and learning behaviours, measuring progress, predicting future attainment, setting targets and ensuring continuity and progression
- Explains how to interpret national initiatives on data-analysis, benchmarking and target-setting, and to ensure that these have value in the classroom

Book 13: *Closing the Learning Gap* by Mike Hughes
ISBN 1-85539-051-5   £15.95

- Helps teachers, departments and schools to close the Learning Gap between what we know about effective learning and what actually goes on in the classroom
- Encourages teachers to reflect on the ways in which they teach, and to identify and implement strategies for improving their practice
- Helps teachers to apply recent research findings about the brain and learning
- Full of practical advice and real, tested strategies for improvement
- Written by a teacher, for teachers, to stimulate thought and interest 'at a glance'

Please note that the prices given above are guaranteed until January 1st, 2000